Digital Detoxification

Embrace Balance, Presence, and Purpose in a Tech-Driven World

Elena Harper

Table of Contents

Introduction

Introduction: Reclaiming Your Life in a Digital World

In a world where we are constantly bombarded with notifications, emails, and an endless stream of social media updates, the idea of stepping away from our devices may seem radical—even impossible. Yet, the overwhelming presence of technology in our daily lives comes with a price: fragmented attention, diminished human connection, and a pervasive sense of exhaustion.

Why a Digital Detox is Essential in Today's Hyper-Connected Era

The Cost of Constant Connectivity

The digital world offers convenience and entertainment but often at the expense of our well-being. Studies show that excessive screen time is linked to increased levels of anxiety, depression, and sleep disturbances. Social media platforms, designed to keep us engaged, amplify feelings of inadequacy and comparison, pulling us into a cycle of consumption that leaves little room for reflection or genuine connection.

Think about how many hours you spend on your devices each day. The average adult checks their phone over 96 times daily, equating to nearly four hours of screen time. Imagine what you could accomplish—mentally, emotionally, and physically— with even half that time redirected toward meaningful pursuits.

The Hidden Impact on Our Relationships

The constant need to stay connected digitally has ironically disconnected us from the people around us. Dinner tables are littered with glowing screens, intimate conversations are interrupted by pings, and family time often involves everyone absorbed in their own digital bubbles. A digital detox can reintroduce the joy of undistracted connection, fostering deeper bonds with loved ones.

The Myth of Multitasking

Technology often convinces us that we can handle everything at once: respond to an email, scroll through Instagram, and listen to a podcast simultaneously. Yet, research consistently proves that multitasking erodes productivity and focus, leaving us more distracted and less efficient. A digital detox is not about rejecting technology but about reclaiming our ability to concentrate and engage deeply.

The Battle for Attention

Modern technology is built to demand your attention. Every app, notification, and algorithm is engineered to keep you hooked—turning your time and focus into a commodity. The competition for your attention is relentless, and without deliberate effort, you risk losing control of one of your most valuable resources: your mental energy. A digital detox gives you the power to take back control, allowing you to prioritize what truly matters.

Rediscovering Joy and Presence

When was the last time you sat quietly and enjoyed a moment without the urge to check your phone? A digital detox isn't just about unplugging; it's about rediscovering the beauty of being fully present. Whether it's savoring a meal, taking a walk in nature, or engaging in a heartfelt conversation, stepping away from screens allows you to immerse yourself in experiences that nourish the soul.

Setting the Stage for Transformation

Embarking on a digital detox is not about deprivation—it's about empowerment. By reducing your reliance on devices, you create space for personal growth, creativity, and authentic connection. This book will guide you through practical steps to regain balance, offering strategies to declutter your digital life and establish a healthier relationship with technology.

In this hyper-connected era, the question isn't whether you should unplug but rather: can you afford not to? A digital detox isn't just a trend; it's a pathway to reclaiming your life, your time, and your peace of mind. Let's begin this journey together.

The science behind screen addiction and its impact on mental health

In the modern age, screens have become an integral part of daily life, connecting us to information, entertainment, and each other. Yet, this constant exposure is reshaping how our brains function, with profound consequences for our mental health. Understanding the science behind screen addiction helps us recognize its effects and take control of our digital habits.

How Screen Addiction Develops

Screen addiction is rooted in the brain's reward system. Every like, notification, or scroll activates the release of dopamine—a neurotransmitter associated with pleasure and reward. Over time, the brain begins to crave these dopamine hits, driving compulsive behaviors similar to substance addiction. This cycle is reinforced as platforms and apps are designed to maximize engagement, keeping users hooked through endless content feeds and unpredictable rewards.

Key Factors Contributing to Screen Addiction:

1. **Variable Rewards:** Much like slot machines, scrolling through social media or notifications offers unpredictable outcomes, creating a "just one more" mentality.

2. **Fear of Missing Out (FOMO):** The psychological urge to stay connected and updated intensifies screen use, creating anxiety when separated from devices.

3. **Social Validation:** Notifications, likes, and comments serve as digital affirmations, reinforcing the desire to remain online.

The Neurological Impact of Excessive Screen Time

Excessive screen time alters brain structure and function, particularly in areas responsible for attention, memory, and emotional regulation.

1. **Reduced Attention Span:** Continuous multitasking between apps and platforms fragments focus, leading to difficulties in maintaining attention on a single task.

2. **Impaired Cognitive Development:** Studies suggest that excessive screen exposure in children can hinder the development of critical thinking, problem-solving, and social skills.

3. **Sleep Disruption:** Blue light emitted by screens suppresses melatonin production, delaying sleep onset and reducing sleep quality, which exacerbates mental health issues.

Mental Health Consequences

1. **Anxiety and Depression:** Constant comparisons on social media often lead to feelings of inadequacy, loneliness, and depression. The pressure to curate a perfect online persona can further fuel anxiety.

2. **Stress and Burnout:** The expectation to always be "online" blurs the boundaries between work and

personal life, resulting in heightened stress levels and eventual burnout.

3. **Isolation and Loneliness:** Paradoxically, while screens connect us globally, they can isolate us locally. Over-reliance on digital communication often replaces face-to-face interactions, weakening real-world relationships.

4. **Addictive Behaviors:** Just like traditional addictions, screen dependency can lead to withdrawal symptoms, such as irritability, restlessness, and mood swings when devices are unavailable.

The Role of Technology Design in Addiction

Tech companies invest heavily in psychological research to make their platforms more engaging. Features such as infinite scrolling, autoplay videos, and algorithm-driven feeds are tailored to exploit human behavior. While these innovations enhance user experience, they also intensify screen dependency, making it harder to disconnect.

Breaking the Cycle

Recognizing the impact of screen addiction is the first step toward change. Understanding the science behind our behaviors empowers us to take proactive measures, such as setting boundaries, practicing mindfulness, and engaging in digital detox strategies. By doing so, we can mitigate the harmful effects of screen addiction and restore balance to our mental well-being.

The Takeaway:

Screen addiction isn't just about overusing devices; it's a neurological and psychological challenge shaped by technology's design and our brain's reward systems.

Addressing it is not just a lifestyle choice—it's essential for preserving mental health in a digital age.

A roadmap to a balanced relationship with technology

In today's world, technology is indispensable—yet its unchecked use can disrupt our mental health, relationships, and productivity. Building a balanced relationship with technology requires a conscious approach that prioritizes your well-being over digital distractions. This roadmap provides actionable steps and insights into how you can coexist harmoniously with technology, leveraging its benefits without falling victim to its pitfalls.

Step 1: Understand the Science Behind Screen Addiction

To develop a balanced relationship with technology, you must first recognize its impact on your brain and behavior. Screen addiction, much like substance addiction, alters the brain's reward system. Here's how:

1. **Dopamine Dependency:** Each notification, like, or message triggers a burst of dopamine—a feel-good chemical that keeps you coming back for more. Over time, your brain associates screen interactions with instant gratification, creating a cycle of dependence.

2. **Cognitive Overload:** Multitasking between apps, emails, and notifications fragments your attention, reducing your ability to concentrate deeply.

3. **Emotional Drain:** Social media fosters constant comparison, contributing to feelings of inadequacy, anxiety, and depression.

Awareness of these effects is the foundation for change. By understanding the science, you can identify habits that hinder your mental health and take deliberate steps to mitigate them.

Step 2: Conduct a Digital Audit

Take stock of your digital habits to identify patterns that may be contributing to screen addiction. Consider the following:

- **Time Tracking:** Use apps like Screen Time (iOS) or Digital Wellbeing (Android) to monitor how much time you spend on your devices and which apps dominate your usage.

- **Emotional Impact:** Reflect on how certain apps or activities make you feel. Are you energized after scrolling social media, or do you feel drained and anxious?

- **Productivity Assessment:** Evaluate whether your screen time aligns with your personal and professional goals or detracts from them.

This audit serves as a diagnostic tool, helping you pinpoint areas that need adjustment.

Step 3: Set Clear Boundaries

Healthy boundaries are essential for fostering a balanced relationship with technology. Here's how to establish them:

1. **Designate Screen-Free Zones:** Create physical spaces in your home, such as the dining table or bedroom, where devices are not allowed.

2. **Set Usage Limits:** Use timers or app restrictions to cap daily usage for non-essential apps.

3. **Schedule Device-Free Hours:** Dedicate time each day to unplug, whether during meals, family time, or a morning routine.

Step 4: Embrace Intentionality in Tech Use

Instead of mindlessly consuming digital content, approach technology with purpose. This involves:

- **Curating Your Feeds:** Unfollow accounts that promote negativity or comparison and replace them with those that inspire, educate, or uplift.

- **Batching Digital Tasks:** Group similar activities, like checking emails or replying to messages, into designated time slots to minimize constant interruptions.

- **Prioritizing Offline Activities:** Replace screen time with hobbies, exercise, or face-to-face interactions that enrich your life.

Step 5: Reclaim Focus with Mindful Practices

The endless stream of digital distractions erodes your ability to focus. Rebuild it through mindfulness:

- **Single-Tasking:** Train your brain to focus on one task at a time instead of multitasking.

- **Digital Meditation:** Use apps like Headspace or Calm to practice mindfulness and counteract the overstimulation caused by screens.

- **Nature Therapy:** Spend time outdoors to reset your mind and break the digital cycle.

Step 6: Leverage Technology to Manage Technology

Paradoxically, technology can help you maintain balance. Use tools designed to minimize screen dependency:

- **Screen Time Management Apps:** Applications like Freedom or RescueTime help limit distractions and track productivity.

- **Wellness Gadgets:** Devices like blue light-blocking glasses or apps with dark mode can reduce eye strain and improve sleep quality.

- **Digital Detox Challenges:** Join programs that encourage unplugging for specific durations to reset your habits.

Step 7: Reflect and Adjust

Achieving a balanced relationship with technology is an ongoing process. Regularly reflect on your progress and make adjustments as needed. Questions to ask yourself include:

- Am I using technology to enhance or escape my life?

- Are my current habits aligning with my long-term goals?

- Do I feel more present, productive, and peaceful?

By continually evaluating and fine-tuning your approach, you can sustain a healthier relationship with technology over time.

Conclusion: Balance Is Key

Technology itself is not the enemy—it's how we use it that matters. A balanced relationship with technology allows you to enjoy its benefits while protecting your mental health and reclaiming your time. By following this roadmap, you can harness technology as a tool for empowerment rather than allowing it to dominate your life. Remember: the goal isn't to eliminate technology but to integrate it in a way that serves your highest priorities.

Chapter 1: The Digital Overload Epidemic

Modern devices and platforms have fundamentally reshaped the way we engage with the world. While they bring unprecedented convenience and connectivity, they are also designed to dominate our attention. The subtle mechanisms that keep us scrolling, clicking, and consuming often go unnoticed but are deeply rooted in psychological tactics and technological innovation.

At the heart of this epidemic lies an economy driven by attention. In the digital age, your focus is a commodity, bought and sold by tech giants. Platforms invest billions in understanding human behavior to create interfaces and algorithms that maximize engagement. Every notification, like, and recommendation is meticulously designed to keep you hooked.

Consider the infinite scroll—a seemingly harmless feature. By removing the natural stopping point of turning a page or ending a feed, this design ensures users continue to consume content without pausing to reflect. Similarly, autoplay for videos creates a passive viewing experience, eliminating the need for conscious decisions and pulling users deeper into the content cycle.

These design choices are not accidents. They exploit the brain's reward system, particularly the dopamine-driven loop that reinforces behaviors associated with pleasure. The unpredictability of what comes next—whether it's a new post, an unexpected message, or a viral video—creates a compulsion to keep checking. This psychological phenomenon mirrors gambling, where intermittent rewards are the most addictive.

The constant bombardment of stimuli fragments our ability to focus. Studies show that the average person checks their phone every few minutes, often without a clear purpose. This habitual checking disrupts deep work, diminishes creativity, and fosters a sense of restlessness. Over time, it trains the brain to seek constant stimulation, making moments of quiet reflection increasingly rare.

Moreover, the competition for attention is relentless. Every app, platform, and device fights to become indispensable in your daily routine. Social media platforms, in particular, tap into fundamental human desires for connection and validation, leveraging likes, comments, and shares as virtual currency. Notifications act as powerful triggers, creating a Pavlovian response that makes it nearly impossible to ignore a buzzing phone.

The consequences of this overload are far-reaching. Productivity suffers as focus is repeatedly interrupted, relationships are strained by divided attention, and mental health takes a hit from the constant comparison and overstimulation inherent in digital interactions. As our brains adapt to this new norm, we risk losing the ability to engage deeply with people, ideas, and experiences.

Understanding how modern devices and platforms hijack your attention is the first step toward regaining control. By recognizing the tactics at play, you can begin to set boundaries, make intentional choices, and reclaim your ability to focus on what truly matters.

Identifying the hidden costs of constant connectivity: productivity, relationships, and health.

While the digital age has brought convenience and efficiency, the hidden costs of constant connectivity often go unnoticed. These costs are not just financial but deeply impact productivity, relationships, and overall health. Recognizing and addressing these consequences is essential for cultivating a balanced, fulfilling life.

The Toll on Productivity

Constant connectivity blurs the line between work and personal time, creating an illusion of multitasking efficiency. However, research consistently shows that switching between tasks—often prompted by notifications or the temptation to check devices—significantly reduces productivity. Each interruption requires time to refocus, leading to what experts call "attention residue."

Emails, instant messages, and social media notifications demand immediate attention, fostering a reactive work style that prioritizes urgency over importance. Over time, this reactive cycle diminishes the ability to engage in deep, focused work, undermining creativity and problem-solving skills. Additionally, digital distractions often lead to longer working hours, leaving less time for rest and personal growth, further compounding the productivity crisis.

Strain on Relationships

Constant connectivity comes with the paradox of being perpetually available yet emotionally distant. While devices enable us to stay in touch with loved ones, they can also erode the quality of those interactions.

Imagine a family dinner where everyone is engrossed in their screens instead of engaging in meaningful conversations. This scenario is increasingly common and highlights how technology can create emotional barriers. The presence of devices during social interactions, even when not in use, reduces feelings of closeness and trust, a phenomenon known as "phubbing" (phone snubbing).

Social media, though designed to connect, often amplifies feelings of inadequacy and jealousy. Curated highlight reels from others' lives can lead to comparisons that strain relationships, fostering resentment or insecurity. Moreover, the compulsive need to document and share moments often detracts from the actual experience, making connections feel superficial.

Impact on Health

The health costs of constant connectivity extend beyond eye strain and bad posture. Persistent digital engagement disrupts the body's natural rhythms and mental well-being.

1. **Sleep Deprivation:** The blue light emitted by screens suppresses melatonin production, delaying the onset of sleep. Coupled with the mental stimulation from late-night scrolling, this results in shorter, poorer-quality sleep, affecting mood, memory, and immune function.

2. **Increased Stress Levels:** The expectation to always be "on" can lead to chronic stress. Whether it's responding to late-night work emails or managing the barrage of notifications, the inability to disconnect creates a state of constant alertness. Over time, this stress contributes to burnout and mental exhaustion.

3. **Mental Health Challenges:** Constant connectivity fuels anxiety and depression. Social media plays a significant role by encouraging endless comparisons and fostering feelings of inadequacy. The dopamine-driven cycle of validation—likes, shares, and comments—can lead to addictive behaviors, further exacerbating mental health struggles.

4. **Physical Inactivity:** Hours spent in front of screens contribute to a sedentary lifestyle, increasing the risk of obesity, cardiovascular issues, and musculoskeletal problems. The absence of physical activity is compounded by the addictive nature of digital platforms, making it difficult to prioritize movement and exercise.

The Cost of Ignoring the Problem

Unchecked, the hidden costs of constant connectivity can spiral into long-term consequences, affecting every aspect of life. Productivity declines as distractions mount, relationships weaken under the weight of divided attention, and health deteriorates due to stress and inactivity.

The good news is that awareness is the first step toward change. By identifying these costs, individuals can take deliberate actions to set boundaries, disconnect intentionally, and prioritize meaningful engagement over constant availability. In doing so, they can reclaim their time, nurture relationships, and protect their mental and physical health.

Real-life stories of people overwhelmed by digital excess

The impact of digital excess is often best understood through the personal experiences of those who have felt its weight. These real-life stories shed light on the struggles and consequences of living in a world dominated by screens—and the lessons learned from reclaiming balance.

Emma: The Burnt-Out Executive

Emma, a 35-year-old marketing executive, prided herself on being always available for her team. Her phone never left her side, and emails, texts, and notifications dictated her every move. She often worked late into the night, answering client queries and managing projects from her bed.

At first, this constant connectivity seemed like an asset, making her indispensable at work. But over time, Emma began experiencing symptoms of burnout: chronic fatigue, anxiety, and irritability. Her relationships suffered as she prioritized digital tasks over time with family and friends. Her partner voiced frustration about her lack of presence during dinner and her habit of checking emails during conversations.

The breaking point came when Emma forgot her niece's birthday, a consequence of being buried in a work-related crisis. Feeling immense guilt, she decided to take a step back. Emma implemented a digital detox strategy, setting work boundaries and rediscovering hobbies like painting. Today, she credits these changes for restoring her mental health and improving her relationships.

Liam: The Social Media Spiral

Liam, a 22-year-old college student, turned to social media during a period of loneliness. Initially, platforms like Instagram and TikTok provided entertainment and a sense of connection. But over time, Liam found himself spending hours scrolling through curated images of his peers' seemingly perfect lives.

This constant exposure to idealized lifestyles triggered feelings of inadequacy. Liam began comparing his academic struggles and part-time job to others' vacation photos and achievements. Despite knowing that social media often presented a distorted reality, he couldn't shake the belief that he was falling behind.

The spiral deepened as Liam started posting more frequently, chasing likes and comments for validation. However, the short-lived satisfaction from these interactions only heightened his anxiety. Recognizing the impact on his mental health, Liam took a bold step: he deleted his social media accounts for a month.

The break allowed him to focus on building real-life connections and rediscovering his self-worth beyond digital affirmations.

Sophia: The Distracted Parent

Sophia, a mother of two young children, struggled to balance the demands of parenting with her growing dependence on her smartphone. Her day revolved around managing her family while staying updated on social media, news, and online shopping deals.

One afternoon, Sophia's five-year-old daughter, Mia, asked her to play a board game. Engrossed in replying to a text, Sophia absentmindedly agreed but failed to engage fully. Mia eventually said, "Mommy, you love your phone more than me." The innocent remark hit Sophia hard, forcing her to reflect on how often her children saw her staring at a screen.

Determined to make a change, Sophia introduced "screen-free family hours" in her household. She began leaving her phone in another room during playtime and started journaling offline to unwind. The result was a stronger bond with her kids and a renewed sense of presence in their lives.

Ryan: The Gamer's Dilemma

Ryan, a 28-year-old software developer, found solace in online gaming after long days at work. What started as a fun escape turned into an all-consuming habit. Ryan spent hours every evening gaming, often skipping meals and sleep to level up or participate in online tournaments.

His social life dwindled as he turned down invitations to spend time with friends. He noticed his work performance slipping, with missed deadlines and a lack of focus during meetings. When his boss commented on his declining productivity, Ryan realized his gaming addiction was jeopardizing his career.

Seeking help, Ryan joined a support group for gamers and set strict limits on his screen time. He also replaced late-night gaming with physical activities like running and joined a local board game club to foster offline connections. This shift helped him regain control over his life and rekindle his passion for coding.

Maya: The Multi-Tasking Mompreneur

Maya, a 40-year-old entrepreneur, managed her business entirely online. Between client emails, social media marketing, and tracking orders on her e-commerce platform, her day was consumed by screens. Even her downtime was filled with browsing Pinterest for inspiration or streaming shows to "unwind."

The constant multitasking left Maya feeling scattered. She struggled to be present with her family and often found herself snapping at her kids when interrupted. Her health began to decline, with frequent headaches and difficulty sleeping.

After attending a workshop on digital wellness, Maya recognized the need to prioritize her well-being. She implemented time-blocking to separate work and personal time and scheduled screen-free evenings for family bonding. Over time, she noticed improvements in her focus, energy, and relationships.

These stories highlight the pervasive impact of digital excess on productivity, relationships, and health. They also remind us that recovery is possible with intentional changes. Each person's journey underscores the importance of awareness, boundaries, and reconnecting with the offline world to reclaim a sense of balance and purpose.

Chapter 2: The Psychology of Digital Addiction

Digital addiction is not a flaw in willpower—it's a carefully engineered phenomenon designed to exploit human psychology. By understanding the forces at play, such as dopamine responses, the fear of missing out (FOMO), and habit loops, you can begin to take control of your digital habits and reclaim your focus.

The Dopamine Connection: The Brain's Reward System

At the core of digital addiction lies dopamine, a neurotransmitter responsible for pleasure and reward. Each notification, like, or message triggers a small surge of dopamine in the brain. This creates a momentary sense of satisfaction, encouraging you to repeat the behavior.

Unlike predictable rewards, the rewards on digital platforms are intermittent—you don't know when you'll get a new like, message, or exciting post. This uncertainty amplifies the dopamine response, making the behavior far more addictive. The brain craves the next hit, prompting endless scrolling and compulsive checking of devices.

Social media platforms, gaming apps, and even news sites capitalize on this cycle. Algorithms prioritize content that is likely to engage you, creating a feedback loop where the more you interact, the more tailored and enticing the content becomes. This isn't accidental—it's intentional design aimed at keeping you hooked.

FOMO: The Fear of Missing Out

FOMO is another powerful driver of digital addiction. It's the psychological fear that you're being left out of something important—whether it's a trending topic, a friend's vacation update, or an invitation to an event.

Social media amplifies FOMO by curating highlight reels of other people's lives. You see only the best moments, not the mundane or challenging ones. This creates an illusion that others are always happier, more successful, or more adventurous than you, prompting you to stay online to "keep up."

FOMO also extends to work and professional settings. Many people feel compelled to respond to emails or check work messages late into the night, fearing they'll miss a critical update or fall behind their colleagues. This constant vigilance adds to the mental load, further entrenching digital habits.

The Habit Loop: Cue, Routine, Reward

Digital behaviors are often reinforced through habit loops, a concept popularized by behavioral psychologists. A habit loop consists of three components:

1. **Cue:** This is the trigger that prompts a behavior. For digital habits, cues often take the form of notifications, boredom, or even stress.

2. **Routine:** The behavior itself—checking your phone, scrolling social media, or playing a game.

3. **Reward:** The sense of satisfaction or relief that follows, such as seeing a new comment, finding a funny meme, or feeling connected.

These loops are powerful because they require minimal conscious effort. Over time, they become automatic, with the brain associating specific cues with specific behaviors. For example, hearing a notification ding may immediately compel you to check your phone, even if you're in the middle of a conversation or task.

The Escalation Effect: Tolerance and Overuse

As with other forms of addiction, the brain builds a tolerance to digital stimulation. What once felt rewarding—receiving a single like or reading a single post—no longer satisfies. This leads to increased consumption, whether through longer screen time, more frequent checks, or seeking out new platforms.

This escalation has significant consequences. More time spent online means less time for meaningful, offline activities. It also reinforces the habit loop, making it harder to break free.

The Role of Personal Triggers

While dopamine, FOMO, and habit loops create a foundation for digital addiction, personal triggers often deepen it. Stress, loneliness, and boredom are common emotions that drive people to their screens for distraction or comfort. Digital platforms offer an easy escape, but the relief is temporary and often exacerbates the underlying issue.

For instance, a stressful day at work might prompt you to binge-watch videos or endlessly scroll social media. While this may offer a short-term distraction, it often leaves you feeling more fatigued or disconnected than before.

Breaking the Cycle

Understanding the psychology behind why we scroll is the first step toward breaking free from digital addiction. Here are some actionable strategies:

- **Identify Your Cues:** Pay attention to what triggers your digital habits. Is it boredom, a notification, or the need for validation?

- **Replace the Routine:** Instead of checking your phone, try engaging in a healthier activity, like journaling, stretching, or taking a short walk.

- **Reevaluate the Reward:** Reflect on whether the reward you're seeking—connection, relaxation, or entertainment—is truly being fulfilled by your screen time. If not, consider alternative ways to achieve that goal.

By understanding how dopamine, FOMO, and habit loops interact to shape your digital behaviors, you can take proactive steps to break free from the grip of addiction. Armed with this knowledge, you'll be better equipped to create healthier habits and reclaim your time and attention.

Tech company tactics: How algorithms keep you hooked

Modern technology is not just a tool—it's a sophisticated system designed to capture and hold your attention. At the heart of this system are algorithms, mathematical models that determine what you see, how often you see it, and how engaging it is. These algorithms are not neutral; they are meticulously crafted by tech companies to keep you hooked for as long as possible.

Understanding these tactics is crucial if you want to break free from the grip of constant connectivity and reclaim control over your digital habits.

Personalization: Curated Just for You

One of the most powerful tactics employed by tech companies is personalization. Algorithms analyze your behavior—what you like, comment on, share, and linger on—to create a digital profile unique to you. This profile drives the content you're shown, ensuring it aligns with your interests and keeps you engaged.

For example, social media platforms like Instagram and TikTok use algorithms to serve content that matches your past behavior, whether it's your favorite types of videos, trending memes, or posts from specific accounts. While this makes the experience enjoyable and relevant, it also creates an echo chamber, reinforcing your habits and keeping you scrolling.

The Infinite Scroll: No End in Sight

The infinite scroll feature, popularized by platforms like Facebook and Twitter, removes natural stopping points. Traditionally, reaching the end of a page would prompt users to pause, reflect, or move on. Infinite scroll, however, keeps the content flowing seamlessly, eliminating those moments of decision-making.

This design capitalizes on a psychological principle known as "loss aversion." The fear of missing out on something important compels users to continue scrolling, even when they know it's unproductive. The result? Hours lost to an endless stream of posts, articles, and videos.

Autoplay: Passive Consumption Made Easy

Video streaming platforms like YouTube and Netflix use autoplay to reduce friction and encourage binge-watching. Once a video ends, the next one starts automatically, often tailored to your viewing history.

Autoplay taps into the brain's preference for ease and convenience. By removing the need to make a choice, it creates a passive consumption loop where you continue watching without realizing how much time has passed. This tactic increases screen time while making it harder to stop.

Notifications: The Digital Tug

Notifications are one of the most direct ways tech companies keep you engaged. Whether it's a new message, a social media like, or a breaking news alert, notifications are designed to capture your attention instantly.

These alerts work on the psychological principle of "intermittent reinforcement," where unpredictable rewards are more addictive than predictable ones. You don't know if the notification will be something exciting or mundane, but the possibility of it being significant triggers a compulsion to check.

Social Validation Loops: The Power of Likes and Shares

Social media platforms leverage our innate desire for social validation. Likes, comments, and shares provide immediate feedback, creating a sense of accomplishment and connection.

However, this validation is fleeting, prompting users to seek it repeatedly. Algorithms amplify this behavior by prioritizing content that is more likely to generate engagement, such as controversial posts or emotionally charged updates. This not only keeps you hooked but also encourages behaviors that align with the platform's metrics of success.

Gamification: Turning Engagement into a Game

Many platforms incorporate gamification elements to make their interfaces more engaging. These include streaks, badges, and achievements. For example, Snapchat's "Snap Streaks" reward users for consistent communication, fostering a sense of obligation to maintain the streak.

This gamified approach triggers a sense of competition or responsibility, compelling users to engage even when they don't genuinely want to.

FOMO Tactics: The Fear of Missing Out

Tech companies amplify FOMO by highlighting what others are doing or what's trending. Features like Instagram Stories or

Twitter's trending topics are ephemeral, meaning they disappear after a set time. This creates urgency, encouraging users to check in frequently to avoid missing out.

Additionally, platforms often notify you about your friends' activities—such as "Your friend just posted for the first time in a while!"—to nudge you into logging back in.

Content Rabbit Holes: One Click Leads to Another

Platforms like YouTube and Reddit use algorithms to suggest content that keeps you engaged for as long as possible. These recommendations are not random; they're based on what has previously kept users like you on the platform.

This tactic leads to "rabbit holes," where one video or post leads to another, often spiraling into hours of unintended consumption. This is particularly common with emotionally charged or controversial content, which algorithms prioritize for its high engagement potential.

Data-Driven Addiction

Tech companies collect vast amounts of data to refine their algorithms continually. Every click, scroll, and pause is analyzed to better predict what will keep you engaged. This data-driven approach ensures that platforms become more addictive over time, adapting to your habits and preferences with increasing precision.

The Cost of Staying Hooked

While these tactics succeed in maximizing user engagement, they come at a significant cost: reduced productivity, strained relationships, and mental health challenges. The constant cycle of dopamine hits and validation loops can lead to addiction, anxiety, and feelings of inadequacy.

Taking Back Control

Breaking free from these tactics starts with awareness. By recognizing how algorithms manipulate your behavior, you can take deliberate steps to reclaim your time and attention. Simple actions like disabling notifications, setting app limits, or consciously pausing after each scroll can disrupt the cycle and help you regain control over your digital habits.

Tech companies may design their platforms to keep you hooked, but you have the power to choose how and when to engage. Reclaiming that choice is the first step toward a healthier relationship with technology.

Recognizing the signs of digital dependency

Digital dependency doesn't develop overnight—it creeps into daily life through subtle habits and behaviors that become deeply ingrained. Recognizing the signs of digital dependency is the first step toward addressing it. By becoming aware of the red flags, you can take proactive steps to regain balance and prioritize your well-being.

1. Excessive Screen Time

Spending long hours on devices is one of the most obvious signs of digital dependency. If you find yourself checking your phone first thing in the morning, scrolling social media during meals, or losing track of time while online, you may be overly reliant on screens.

- **Red Flag:** Feeling surprised or guilty when you realize how much time has passed while using your device.

- **Reality Check:** Studies suggest that the average person spends over 7 hours a day on screens, often unintentionally.

2. Difficulty Disconnecting

A common sign of digital dependency is the inability to stay offline for extended periods. If the thought of being without your phone or internet access causes anxiety or discomfort, it's a clear indication that you've grown dependent.

- **Red Flag:** Feeling "phantom vibrations" or constantly checking your phone, even when there are no notifications.

- **Reality Check:** This behavior stems from the brain's craving for the dopamine hit associated with notifications or messages.

3. Neglecting Real-World Responsibilities

When digital activities take precedence over daily tasks or responsibilities, it's a sign that your online habits are interfering with your life. This could include procrastinating on work, skipping meals, or forgoing physical activity in favor of screen time.

- **Red Flag:** Regularly telling yourself, "Just five more minutes," only to spend hours online instead of completing important tasks.

- **Reality Check:** Digital dependency often leads to declining productivity and unfulfilled obligations.

4. Reduced Attention Span

Constant exposure to quick, bite-sized content—like social media posts or short videos—conditions your brain to seek instant gratification. This can make it difficult to focus on longer, more meaningful tasks.

- **Red Flag:** Struggling to read a book, complete a project, or sit through a meeting without checking your phone.

- **Reality Check:** Research shows that heavy tech use is linked to a declining ability to sustain focus and engage in deep work.

5. Social Isolation

Ironically, while technology is designed to connect us, excessive use often leads to isolation. If you find yourself prioritizing online interactions over face-to-face connections, your digital habits may be negatively impacting your social life.

- **Red Flag:** Opting to text or scroll social media rather than engage in real-world conversations.

- **Reality Check:** True connection requires more than likes and comments; it needs meaningful, in-person interaction.

6. Mood Swings Linked to Online Activity

Your emotional state may become tied to what happens online. This includes feeling elated when receiving likes and comments or feeling irritable, anxious, or depressed when you don't.

- **Red Flag:** Checking social media makes you feel stressed or inadequate, yet you can't stop.

- **Reality Check:** Social media's curated content often amplifies feelings of comparison and inadequacy, fueling dependency.

7. Compromised Sleep Patterns

The blue light emitted by screens disrupts your body's natural sleep-wake cycle, making it harder to fall asleep. If you regularly stay up late scrolling or wake up feeling unrested, your digital habits may be interfering with your sleep.

- **Red Flag:** Falling asleep with your phone in hand or waking up multiple times during the night to check notifications.

- **Reality Check:** Poor sleep due to screen time can lead to fatigue, reduced cognitive function, and a weakened immune system.

8. Anxiety When Offline

Feeling restless, irritable, or anxious when you're away from your device is a hallmark of digital dependency. This "withdrawal" indicates that your brain has become accustomed to constant digital stimulation.

- **Red Flag:** Frequently reaching for your phone during downtime, even when there's nothing to check.

- **Reality Check:** The fear of missing out (FOMO) and a conditioned need for connection drive this anxiety.

9. Loss of Interest in Offline Activities

Hobbies and activities you once enjoyed may lose their appeal as you increasingly turn to digital alternatives. Whether it's reading, exercising, or spending time outdoors, these activities may feel less satisfying compared to the instant gratification of screen-based entertainment.

- **Red Flag:** Skipping offline plans or feeling bored without a device in hand.

- **Reality Check:** A fulfilling life requires a balance between online and offline experiences.

10. Physical Symptoms

Digital dependency often manifests in physical symptoms, such as eye strain, headaches, or neck and back pain from prolonged screen use. Additionally, a sedentary lifestyle linked to excessive device use can contribute to weight gain and other health issues.

- **Red Flag:** Experiencing discomfort or fatigue but continuing to stay glued to your screen.

- **Reality Check:** Over time, these physical symptoms can lead to more serious health problems.

What to Do Next

Recognizing these signs is the first step toward breaking free from digital dependency. Reflect on your habits, set boundaries, and take intentional steps to regain control. By limiting screen time, prioritizing offline activities, and fostering meaningful connections, you can reduce dependency and lead a more balanced, intentional life.

Chapter 3: The Benefits of a Digital Detox

In a world dominated by constant connectivity, the idea of a digital detox might feel counterintuitive. Yet, stepping away from screens can have profound and transformative effects on your focus, creativity, and mental clarity. By intentionally disconnecting, you create space to reconnect with your thoughts, passions, and purpose.

Improved Focus: Reclaiming Your Attention

The digital age has trained our brains to crave instant gratification, often at the expense of sustained attention. Notifications, endless scrolling, and multitasking fragment our focus, making it challenging to complete tasks or engage deeply with any one activity.

A digital detox helps reverse this by removing the constant interruptions that hijack your attention. When you unplug, you allow your brain to rebuild its capacity for sustained concentration. This improved focus can lead to:

- **Enhanced Productivity:** With fewer distractions, you can devote uninterrupted time to tasks, completing them more efficiently and with higher quality.

- **Deeper Engagement:** Without the urge to check your phone or refresh your inbox, you can immerse yourself fully in work, hobbies, or conversations.

- **Better Time Management:** By eliminating the hours lost to mindless scrolling, you free up time to prioritize what truly matters.

Creativity Unleashed: Tapping Into Your Inner Genius

Creativity thrives in moments of stillness and boredom—two states that are increasingly rare in the digital age. The constant influx of information from screens leaves little room for original thought or the incubation of ideas.

When you step away from digital distractions, you create a mental "white space" where creativity can flourish. Benefits of a digital detox for creativity include:

- **Increased Imagination:** Disconnecting allows your mind to wander, sparking new ideas and solutions that might not emerge in a cluttered mental state.

- **Deeper Reflection:** With fewer external inputs, you can process your thoughts more effectively, leading to insights and breakthroughs.

- **Rekindled Passions:** Stepping away from screens gives you the opportunity to reconnect with creative hobbies like writing, painting, or playing an instrument, reigniting your sense of joy and purpose.

Mental Clarity: Finding Peace Amid the Noise

Constant connectivity bombards your brain with information, leaving it overstimulated and overwhelmed. This mental clutter can lead to decision fatigue, stress, and a diminished ability to think clearly.

A digital detox acts as a reset button for your mind. By reducing the flow of digital noise, you can achieve:

- **Sharper Decision-Making:** A clearer mind helps you weigh options more effectively, making decisions with confidence and precision.

- **Emotional Balance:** Time away from the often negative influences of social media can improve your mood, reduce anxiety, and foster a sense of calm.

- **Heightened Self-Awareness:** Unplugging allows you to tune into your inner thoughts and emotions, fostering personal growth and self-discovery.

The Ripple Effects of These Benefits

The gains from a digital detox extend far beyond your personal experience. Improved focus, creativity, and mental clarity can enhance every aspect of your life:

- **In Relationships:** You'll be more present and engaged with loved ones, deepening your connections and strengthening your bonds.

- **In Your Career:** Renewed focus and creativity can lead to better performance, innovative thinking, and professional growth.

- **In Your Well-Being:** Mental clarity reduces stress and increases your overall sense of peace, helping you approach life with greater resilience and positivity.

Your Mind, Reimagined

The benefits of a digital detox are not about rejecting technology but about restoring balance. By stepping away from screens, even temporarily, you can unlock your mind's full potential, rediscover your passions, and approach life with renewed focus and intention. Imagine a life where you're not just reacting to the digital world but actively shaping your own path with clarity and creativity. That's the power of a digital detox.

Strengthening personal connections and emotional well-being

In a hyper-connected digital age, genuine human connections often take a backseat to virtual interactions. While technology enables instant communication, it can also dilute the quality of our relationships and erode emotional well-being. Disconnecting from screens, even briefly, can create space for deeper personal connections and foster a renewed sense of emotional balance.

Rediscovering the Power of Presence

One of the greatest casualties of digital overuse is the ability to be fully present. When conversations are interrupted by notifications or eyes wander to screens during family time, relationships suffer. A conscious effort to unplug strengthens personal connections by allowing you to:

- **Engage Actively:** Without distractions, you can truly listen and respond thoughtfully, creating a deeper bond with loved ones.

- **Share Quality Time:** Whether it's a meal, a walk, or a shared hobby, screen-free moments foster meaningful interactions that build lasting memories.

- **Show Genuine Empathy:** Being fully present helps you pick up on non-verbal cues, like body language and tone, enhancing your ability to empathize and connect.

Building Stronger Relationships

Digital detoxing doesn't just improve the quantity of time spent with others; it enhances the quality of those moments. Here's how stepping away from screens can strengthen your relationships:

- **Rekindling Intimacy:** Couples often find that unplugging together improves their communication and brings them closer. Without the interference of devices, they can focus on each other and reconnect on a deeper level.

- **Fostering Deeper Bonds with Family:** Setting aside screen-free time encourages shared activities, such as board games, cooking, or outdoor adventures, which help families reconnect and create lasting traditions.

- **Rebuilding Friendships:** Taking the time to meet friends in person, rather than relying on messages or social media updates, fosters more authentic and fulfilling connections.

Cultivating Emotional Well-Being

Constant exposure to social media and online content often contributes to feelings of inadequacy, anxiety, and stress. The curated highlight reels of others' lives can create unrealistic comparisons, while the 24/7 barrage of news can amplify worry and negativity. Disconnecting from these influences has profound benefits for emotional health:

- **Reducing Stress:** Time away from screens lowers cortisol levels, allowing your body and mind to relax.

- **Boosting Self-Esteem:** Without the pressure to perform or compare, you can focus on appreciating your own unique journey and achievements.

- **Encouraging Mindfulness:** Stepping away from the digital world helps you become more aware of your thoughts, emotions, and surroundings, fostering a sense of calm and clarity.

Strengthening Your Sense of Community

True connection thrives in shared experiences. A digital detox allows you to engage more actively with your local community and social circles:

- **Participating in Local Events:** Joining a book club, attending a yoga class, or volunteering creates opportunities to connect with others face-to-face.

- **Strengthening Support Systems:** Spending more time with close friends and family provides a robust emotional safety net, reducing feelings of loneliness or isolation.

- **Engaging in Meaningful Conversations:** Without the distraction of screens, conversations become richer and more fulfilling, helping you feel more understood and valued.

Modeling Healthy Habits

Your decision to unplug can have a ripple effect on those around you, especially within your family or close social groups. By modeling healthy digital habits, you:

- **Inspire Children to Disconnect:** Encouraging screen-free play and activities teaches kids the value of real-world interactions and creativity.

- **Encourage Friends and Colleagues:** Your intentional choice to focus on personal connections can inspire others to do the same, fostering a culture of mindfulness and presence.

Embracing the Joy of Offline Relationships

The benefits of strengthening personal connections extend beyond the immediate. Deeper bonds and improved emotional well-being provide a foundation for resilience, happiness, and a sense of belonging. By disconnecting from the digital noise, you open yourself to the beauty of human connection—a smile, a shared laugh, a heartfelt conversation—that no screen can replicate.

Strengthening personal connections isn't just about unplugging; it's about plugging into what truly matters: the people who enrich your life and the emotional well-being that comes from being fully present with them.

A healthier, more intentional lifestyle

In the digital age, it's easy to get swept up in the fast-paced rhythm of constant notifications, endless scrolling, and multitasking. However, stepping back and intentionally reshaping how you engage with technology can lead to a healthier, more purposeful way of living. A digital detox is not just about unplugging—it's about reimagining your lifestyle to prioritize balance, well-being, and meaningful choices.

Prioritizing Physical Health

Excessive screen time often leads to a sedentary lifestyle, disrupted sleep patterns, and other health issues. Adopting a healthier approach to technology can positively impact your physical well-being in several ways:

- **Increased Movement:** Without the lure of screens, you can dedicate more time to physical activities like walking, yoga, or hitting the gym, which improve overall fitness and energy levels.

- **Better Sleep Quality:** Reducing screen time before bed minimizes exposure to blue light, allowing your body to produce melatonin naturally and promoting restful sleep.

- **Improved Posture:** Less screen time reduces the strain on your neck, shoulders, and back, alleviating the discomfort caused by "tech neck" and prolonged sitting.

Enhancing Mental Clarity and Emotional Balance

A healthier, more intentional lifestyle also focuses on your mental and emotional health. By minimizing digital distractions, you can create the mental space needed to reflect, recharge, and connect with your inner self.

- **Reduced Stress:** A break from the constant barrage of information and notifications allows your mind to unwind, reducing feelings of overwhelm and anxiety.

- **Improved Self-Awareness:** With fewer distractions, you can better understand your thoughts, emotions, and triggers, fostering personal growth.

- **Increased Emotional Resilience:** Disconnecting from the often toxic or negative aspects of social media can help you develop a more positive and balanced outlook on life.

Fostering Mindfulness

Intentional living is rooted in mindfulness—the practice of being fully present in the moment. A healthier approach to technology can help cultivate this awareness:

- **Being Present:** Without the pull of notifications, you can focus more deeply on the people and activities in front of you.

- **Slowing Down:** Embracing a slower, more intentional pace allows you to savor experiences and make thoughtful choices rather than reacting impulsively.

- **Finding Joy in Simplicity:** Disconnecting from digital excess helps you appreciate life's simple pleasures, like reading a book, enjoying nature, or sharing a meal with loved ones.

Making Time for What Matters

One of the greatest benefits of a healthier, more intentional lifestyle is the ability to prioritize what truly matters. By limiting the time spent on screens, you create more space for meaningful activities:

- **Nurturing Relationships:** Invest in deeper connections with family, friends, and community by engaging in face-to-face interactions and shared experiences.

- **Pursuing Passions:** Rediscover hobbies or creative pursuits that bring you joy, from painting and cooking to gardening and writing.

- **Focusing on Personal Goals:** Use your newfound time and mental energy to work toward long-term goals, whether it's learning a new skill, advancing your career, or improving your health.

Aligning Actions with Values

Living intentionally means aligning your daily choices with your core values and priorities. A healthier relationship with technology can help you:

- **Evaluate Your Priorities:** Reflect on what matters most in your life and make choices that support those priorities.

- **Set Boundaries:** Establish limits on digital use to ensure it supports your goals rather than detracts from them.

- **Live with Purpose:** Each decision becomes more thoughtful, leading to a life that feels meaningful and fulfilling.

The Ripple Effect: Inspiring Others

Your decision to embrace a healthier, more intentional lifestyle can inspire those around you. By modeling balance and mindfulness, you encourage others—friends, family, and colleagues—to rethink their habits and prioritize well-being. Together, these collective changes can create a culture that values presence, purpose, and genuine connection over digital distractions.

The Path Forward

Adopting a healthier, more intentional lifestyle is not about rejecting technology but using it in ways that serve your highest priorities. It's about creating space for what truly matters—your health, relationships, passions, and inner peace.

When you step away from the digital noise and embrace intentional living, you'll find a renewed sense of clarity, fulfillment, and joy. This lifestyle isn't just a choice; it's a commitment to your well-being and the life you deserve.

Chapter 4: Preparing for Your Detox Journey

Embarking on a digital detox journey begins with understanding your current relationship with technology. Awareness is key to making meaningful changes, and a self-audit is the perfect tool to evaluate your digital habits. By taking the time to assess how, when, and why you engage with technology, you can identify areas for improvement and set realistic goals for your detox.

The Importance of a Self-Audit

A self-audit helps you uncover the hidden patterns in your digital usage. It's not about judgment but about understanding. By reflecting on your habits, you gain clarity about how technology affects your time, productivity, relationships, and overall well-being. This insight forms the foundation of a successful digital detox.

Your Self-Audit Worksheet

Use the following prompts to evaluate your digital habits. Be honest and specific in your responses to gain the most accurate picture of your technology use.

Section 1: Time Spent on Devices

1. **How many hours a day do you spend on your phone, computer, or tablet?**

   - Divide this into categories like work, social media, streaming, gaming, and communication.

   - Use apps like Screen Time (iOS) or Digital Wellbeing (Android) to get exact numbers.

2. **What is your first and last interaction with your device each day?**

- For example, do you check emails or scroll social media first thing in the morning or before bed?

3. **How often do you pick up your phone during the day?**

- Note whether these instances are intentional (e.g., responding to work emails) or impulsive (e.g., checking notifications).

Section 2: Purpose of Usage

1. **What are your primary reasons for using technology?**

- Examples might include work, entertainment, staying informed, or connecting with others.

2. **How often do you use technology for productive purposes versus mindless consumption?**

- Productive: Reading an eBook, completing a work task.

- Mindless: Endless scrolling, watching random videos.

3. **Do you frequently multitask while using technology?**

- For example, watching a show while scrolling through your phone.

Section 3: Emotional Impact

1. **How does using technology make you feel?**

- Reflect on emotions like stress, joy, anxiety, boredom, or accomplishment.

2. **Do you notice any negative emotional triggers linked to certain apps or platforms?**

- For instance, feelings of inadequacy from social media or anxiety from constant notifications.

3. **Do you experience withdrawal symptoms when away from your device?**

   - Examples might include restlessness, irritability, or a compulsive urge to check your phone.

Section 4: Impact on Daily Life

1. **Does technology interfere with your relationships?**

   - Consider whether it disrupts conversations, family time, or social activities.

2. **Has screen time affected your productivity at work or school?**

   - For example, procrastinating on tasks or getting distracted by non-essential digital activities.

3. **Do you notice any physical health effects from excessive device use?**

   - Common issues include eye strain, neck pain, or disrupted sleep patterns.

Section 5: Defining Your Goals

1. **What do you hope to achieve from a digital detox?**

   - Examples: Improved focus, stronger relationships, better mental health, or more free time.

2. **Which aspects of your digital habits are you most eager to change?**

- Identify specific behaviors, such as reducing social media usage or limiting device time before bed.

3. **How will you measure success during your detox?**

   - Define clear metrics, such as spending fewer than 2 hours on social media daily or designating screen-free zones.

Interpreting Your Self-Audit

After completing the worksheet, review your responses to identify patterns and problem areas. Ask yourself:

- Which digital habits are adding value to my life?

- Which habits are draining my time, energy, or emotional well-being?

- What small, actionable changes can I implement immediately?

This self-awareness will guide you as you plan your detox journey, helping you set achievable goals and track your progress.

Taking the First Step

Your self-audit is more than just an exercise—it's a commitment to yourself. By honestly evaluating your digital habits, you've taken the critical first step toward regaining control and building a healthier relationship with technology. The next step is to put this knowledge into action, creating a plan that aligns with your goals and lifestyle.

Your digital detox journey starts here, and the insights you've gained from this self-audit will be your compass. Take it one step at a time, and remember: the goal is not perfection but progress toward a more intentional and fulfilling life.

Setting realistic goals and expectations for detoxing

Embarking on a digital detox journey can be transformative, but like any significant change, it requires thoughtful planning and realistic expectations. Setting achievable goals ensures that you maintain motivation and see tangible progress, while also avoiding feelings of overwhelm or failure. A well-structured approach helps you build a sustainable, healthier relationship with technology.

Why Realistic Goals Matter

Unrealistic expectations can derail even the most well-intentioned efforts. Trying to quit all digital activities abruptly or setting rigid rules can lead to frustration or burnout. Instead, realistic goals create a balance between challenge and achievability, making the process both manageable and rewarding.

Steps to Setting Realistic Detox Goals

1. Reflect on Your Motivations

Understanding *why* you want to detox is the foundation for setting meaningful goals. Are you aiming to improve focus, strengthen relationships, or reduce stress? Defining your "why" helps you tailor goals to your priorities.

- **Example Goals:**
    - "I want to reclaim two hours each day to spend with my family."
    - "I need to stop checking my phone during meals to be more present."

2. Start Small for Big Changes

It's tempting to go all-in, but incremental changes are often more effective. Focus on small, specific adjustments rather than sweeping restrictions.

- **Beginner Goals:**
    - Limit social media use to 30 minutes per day.
    - Establish one screen-free hour before bedtime.
    - Designate one day a week as a "no-tech" day.

Gradually build on these changes as you become more comfortable with reduced digital reliance.

3. Focus on What You Can Control

You may not be able to avoid all screen time, especially if your work or studies rely on technology. Instead, set goals around aspects of your digital life that you can control, such as personal screen use or leisure activities.

- **Realistic Expectations:**
    - "I will use my phone for work but avoid checking non-essential apps during office hours."
    - "I will take breaks from my laptop every 90 minutes to stretch and refresh."

4. Define Measurable Outcomes

Clear, measurable goals make it easier to track progress and stay motivated. Avoid vague intentions like "spend less time online" and instead use specific metrics.

- **Examples of Measurable Goals:**

- "Reduce daily screen time from 5 hours to 3 hours within two weeks."

- "Replace 20 minutes of scrolling with reading a physical book each evening."

- "Check emails only twice a day—once in the morning and once in the afternoon."

5. Anticipate Challenges and Plan for Them

Acknowledging potential obstacles helps you prepare realistic solutions. Be honest about habits or situations that might tempt you to revert to old patterns.

- **Common Challenges:**
  - Boredom during downtime.
  - The urge to check notifications.
  - Pressure from work or social expectations to stay connected.

- **Actionable Strategies:**
  - Keep a list of offline activities to fill idle moments, such as journaling, exercising, or cooking.
  - Turn off non-essential notifications to reduce interruptions.
  - Communicate your detox goals with friends, family, or colleagues to set expectations.

6. Balance Restrictions with Rewards

A successful detox doesn't mean eliminating technology entirely—it's about creating a balance. Set boundaries for screen use while still allowing for moments of intentional engagement.

- **Balanced Goals:**
    - o "I will check social media for 10 minutes after completing a morning workout."
    - o "I will enjoy one episode of my favorite show after spending time outdoors."

Using rewards as incentives helps reinforce positive habits without making the detox feel like deprivation.

7. Be Flexible and Forgiving

Progress is rarely linear, and slip-ups are a natural part of the process. Instead of viewing these moments as failures, treat them as learning opportunities.

- **Adaptability Tips:**
    - o If you exceed your screen-time goal, reflect on what triggered the overuse and adjust your strategy.
    - o Celebrate small wins, such as successfully completing a screen-free evening or resisting the urge to check your phone during a meeting.

Remember, the goal is progress, not perfection.

Setting Expectations for the Detox Experience

1. Understand That Detoxing Takes Time

Breaking long-standing habits won't happen overnight. Be patient with yourself and focus on gradual improvements. Expect that it may take weeks or even months to fully adjust to reduced screen time.

2. Recognize Emotional Reactions

You may initially feel restless, bored, or even anxious as you reduce your digital interactions. These feelings are normal and typically subside as your brain adapts to the new routine.

- **Tip:** Use these moments as an opportunity to explore offline activities that bring joy or relaxation, such as meditating, hiking, or spending time with loved ones.

3. Expect Pushback

Others around you may not understand or support your digital detox, especially if they're accustomed to your constant availability. Communicate your goals clearly and explain why this process is important to you.

Conclusion: Your Path to Digital Freedom

Setting realistic goals and expectations for your detox journey ensures that you build habits that last. By starting small, staying adaptable, and focusing on progress, you can create a healthier relationship with technology. The key is not to strive for perfection but to embrace the process, knowing that every step forward brings you closer to a more intentional and fulfilling lifestyle.

Enlisting support from family and friends

Embarking on a digital detox can be a personal journey, but having the support of your family and friends can make the process more enjoyable and sustainable. Their involvement not only reinforces your commitment but also creates opportunities for deeper connections and shared growth. Here's how to enlist the help of your loved ones as you navigate this transformative experience.

Why Support Matters

A digital detox often involves breaking ingrained habits and overcoming societal norms around constant connectivity. Family and friends can serve as:

- **Accountability Partners:** Helping you stay committed to your goals and providing gentle reminders when you slip.

- **Motivators:** Encouraging you to keep going, especially during challenging moments.

- **Companions:** Sharing offline activities and fostering a sense of camaraderie during the detox.

Their support can make the journey less isolating and more rewarding.

Steps to Enlist Support

1. Share Your Intentions Clearly

Start by explaining why you've decided to undertake a digital detox. Be open about your goals and the benefits you hope to achieve. Sharing your motivations helps others understand your journey and encourages them to respect your boundaries.

- **Conversation Starters:**
  - "I've realized that my screen time is affecting my focus and relationships, so I'm trying a digital detox to create a better balance."
  - "I want to be more present during our time together, so I'm reducing my phone use."

2. Set Boundaries and Expectations

Let your loved ones know how your detox might change your interactions with them. This could include less texting, fewer social media updates, or designated screen-free times. Be clear about what they can expect from you and ask for their understanding.

- **Examples of Boundaries:**
    - "I won't be checking my phone after 8 PM, so if it's urgent, please call me instead."
    - "During meals, I'd like us to keep our phones away so we can focus on each other."

3. Encourage Participation

Invite your family and friends to join you in the detox, even if only for a short time or specific activities. Making the detox a collective effort can strengthen your bonds and make the process more enjoyable.

- **Group Activities:**
    - Organize a screen-free game night or outdoor picnic.
    - Plan a weekend hike or a tech-free dinner party.
    - Start a shared offline hobby, such as gardening or crafting.

4. Ask for Accountability

Accountability partners can help you stay on track by checking in regularly and offering encouragement. Choose someone who is supportive, understanding, and willing to help you achieve your goals.

- **Accountability Tips:**
    - Share your daily or weekly progress with a friend or family member.

- Agree on a system of reminders or check-ins, such as a quick text or call to see how you're doing.

- Celebrate milestones together, like completing a screen-free day or week.

5. Be Patient with Resistance

Not everyone may immediately understand or support your decision to detox. Some might feel that your reduced online presence affects their ability to reach you, or they may question the necessity of a detox altogether. Address their concerns with empathy and reassurance.

- **How to Respond:**

  - "I'm still here for you, but I'm trying to find a healthier balance with technology."

  - "This isn't about disconnecting from you—it's about reconnecting with myself and the people I care about."

6. Lead by Example

Your commitment to the detox can inspire others to reflect on their own digital habits. By modeling the benefits of unplugging—such as increased focus, better moods, and more meaningful interactions—you may encourage them to adopt similar practices.

- **Visible Changes:**

  - Being fully present during conversations.

  - Sharing stories of offline achievements or experiences.

  - Demonstrating the joy of screen-free activities.

7. Create a Supportive Environment

Work with your family and friends to create an environment that supports your detox goals. This might include:

- **Screen-Free Zones:** Establishing areas in your home, such as the dining table or living room, where devices are not allowed.

- **Shared Detox Goals:** Setting collective goals, like a "no phones during family meals" rule.

- **Offline Alternatives:** Keeping board games, books, or puzzles readily available for shared entertainment.

8. Celebrate Together

Acknowledging and celebrating milestones can keep everyone motivated and invested in the process. Whether it's completing a week-long detox challenge or enjoying an entire day without screens, take time to recognize the progress you've made together.

- **Celebration Ideas:**
    - A family outing to a park or museum.
    - A group dinner where everyone shares their favorite offline moments.
    - A small reward, like treating yourselves to a tech-free spa day or movie night.

Conclusion: Strength in Connection

Enlisting the support of family and friends turns your digital detox from a solo endeavor into a shared experience. Their encouragement and participation not only make the journey easier but also strengthen your relationships along the way. By working together to create a healthier, more intentional lifestyle, you can foster deeper connections and a renewed sense of togetherness—both offline and beyond.

Chapter 5: Crafting Your Digital-Free Space

A successful digital detox starts with a supportive environment. Crafting a digital-free space doesn't just mean putting your phone on silent or turning off the TV—it's about intentionally designing areas in your home or workspace that encourage mindfulness, creativity, and connection. By removing distractions and setting clear boundaries, you create a physical and mental space that supports your goals.

The Importance of a Digital-Free Space

Your environment plays a crucial role in shaping your habits. A cluttered, tech-filled space constantly draws your attention to screens, reinforcing digital dependency. Conversely, a well-designed, tech-free area invites you to focus on meaningful activities, from reading and journaling to spending quality time with loved ones.

Steps to Design Your Digital-Free Space

1. Identify Key Areas for Transformation

Start by pinpointing spaces in your home or office that would benefit from being screen-free. These are typically areas where you want to relax, focus, or connect.

- **Common Digital-Free Zones:**
    - **Bedroom:** To improve sleep and relaxation.
    - **Dining Table:** To encourage mindful eating and meaningful conversations.
    - **Living Room:** To prioritize connection and leisure without screens.
    - **Workspace:** To boost productivity and minimize distractions.

2. Remove Temptations

The first step in crafting a digital-free space is decluttering it of unnecessary tech devices and accessories. Out of sight, out of mind!

- **Actionable Tips:**
  - Relocate chargers and devices to another room to reduce the temptation to check them.
  - Use physical alternatives to digital tools, like an alarm clock instead of a phone or a paper planner instead of a scheduling app.
  - Store gaming consoles or other entertainment devices in cabinets or drawers when not in use.

3. Establish Clear Boundaries

Set clear rules for your digital-free spaces to ensure they remain sanctuaries from screens.

- **Examples of Boundaries:**
  - No phones or laptops allowed in the bedroom after 9 PM.
  - No devices at the dining table during meals.
  - No social media scrolling in the living room.

Enlist the cooperation of family members or roommates to respect these boundaries and help maintain the integrity of the space.

4. Create a Sensory-Friendly Environment

Your digital-free space should be inviting and conducive to relaxation, creativity, or focus. Pay attention to the sensory elements of the space to make it more appealing.

- **Lighting:** Use warm, natural lighting to create a calming atmosphere. Consider candles or dimmable lamps for the evening.

- **Comfort:** Add cozy furniture, cushions, or blankets to make the space feel welcoming.

- **Nature:** Incorporate plants or flowers to bring a touch of the outdoors inside, which can help reduce stress and boost mood.

- **Aromas:** Use essential oils, scented candles, or fresh air to make the space more pleasant.

5. Stock Your Space with Offline Alternatives

Having engaging offline activities readily available makes it easier to resist the pull of screens. Equip your digital-free space with items that align with your interests and goals.

- **Ideas for Your Space:**
    - Books, magazines, or journals.
    - Board games, puzzles, or craft supplies.
    - A yoga mat or meditation cushion for mindfulness practices.
    - Musical instruments or art materials for creative expression.

6. Designate Tech Charging Zones

To maintain the sanctity of your digital-free spaces, create designated tech zones elsewhere in your home. These are areas where devices can be charged or stored without disrupting other parts of your environment.

- **Tech Zone Tips:**
  - Keep charging stations in a central location, like the kitchen or hallway.
  - Use baskets or drawers to organize devices neatly.
  - Set up "parking spots" for phones and tablets during family time or meals.

7. Make It a Shared Effort

If you live with family or roommates, involve them in designing and maintaining digital-free spaces. Their buy-in ensures that everyone respects the boundaries and enjoys the benefits of the environment.

- **Shared Activities in Digital-Free Spaces:**
  - Cook or eat meals together.
  - Play board games or engage in group hobbies.
  - Have open conversations without interruptions.

8. Periodically Refresh the Space

Over time, your digital-free space may need updates to keep it engaging and functional. Periodically assess its effectiveness and make changes as needed.

- **Refresh Ideas:**
  - Rotate books, games, or decorations to keep the space interesting.
  - Rearrange furniture to improve flow or comfort.

o   Add new elements, like a plant or artwork, to enhance the ambiance.

The Benefits of a Digital-Free Space

By creating intentional spaces free from screens, you can experience a range of benefits:

- **Improved Focus:** Reduced distractions allow you to concentrate fully on tasks or hobbies.

- **Enhanced Relaxation:** A calm, screen-free environment fosters peace of mind and reduces stress.

- **Stronger Connections:** Shared digital-free spaces encourage deeper interactions with loved ones.

- **Greater Creativity:** Without the noise of digital distractions, your mind is free to wander and innovate.

Conclusion: A Sanctuary from the Digital World

Crafting a digital-free space is a powerful step toward reclaiming balance in your life. These intentional areas serve as sanctuaries where you can recharge, connect, and engage with the world around you without the interference of screens. By designing your environment for success, you set the stage for lasting habits that promote focus, well-being, and fulfillment.

The power of physical spaces free from screens.

The Power of Physical Spaces Free from Screens

In an era dominated by digital devices, creating physical spaces free from screens is more than just a lifestyle choice—it's a transformative practice that nurtures focus, creativity, and well-being. These screen-free sanctuaries offer a chance to reconnect with yourself, others, and the world around you in meaningful and enriching ways. The power of such spaces lies in their ability to ground you in the present moment and remind you of life's simpler joys.

Fostering Presence and Mindfulness

Physical spaces free from screens invite mindfulness, the practice of being fully present in the here and now. Without the pull of notifications, pings, or the endless scroll, you can immerse yourself in your surroundings and activities.

- **Increased Awareness:** A screen-free environment encourages you to notice the little things—a bird chirping outside, the texture of a book's pages, or the subtle flavors in a meal.

- **Deeper Reflection:** Quiet, tech-free spaces give you the mental clarity to process thoughts, reflect on your day, and gain insights that often get lost in the digital noise.

- **Reduced Stress:** The absence of screens minimizes overstimulation, allowing your body and mind to relax and recharge.

Strengthening Relationships

Screen-free spaces are powerful tools for building stronger personal connections. They create an environment where conversations flow naturally, undisturbed by digital distractions.

- **Improved Communication:** Without devices dividing attention, you can engage in active listening, meaningful conversations, and genuine exchanges of ideas.

- **Shared Moments:** Physical spaces free from screens foster shared activities like cooking together, playing board games, or simply enjoying a walk. These interactions deepen bonds and create lasting memories.

- **Modeling Healthy Habits:** For families, screen-free zones set a positive example for children, teaching them the value of being present and engaged in real-world interactions.

Boosting Creativity and Focus

Screens often fragment attention and dampen creativity, as they bombard the brain with constant input. Screen-free spaces, on the other hand, provide the mental white space necessary for innovation and deep thinking.

- **Unleashing Imagination:** With fewer distractions, your mind can wander freely, sparking new ideas and creative solutions.

- **Enhancing Productivity:** Focused, uninterrupted time in a tech-free zone allows you to tackle tasks with greater efficiency and clarity.

- **Cultivating Hobbies:** Screen-free spaces encourage the pursuit of offline passions, such as painting, writing, gardening, or playing an instrument.

Improving Physical Health

Creating physical spaces free from screens can have a positive impact on your body as well as your mind.

- **Promoting Movement:** Without the temptation to stay seated with a device, you're more likely to engage in physical activities like stretching, walking, or exercising.

- **Protecting Sleep Quality:** Screen-free bedrooms, for instance, eliminate exposure to blue light before bedtime, helping regulate your sleep-wake cycle and improve rest.

- **Reducing Strain:** Limiting screen time can alleviate common issues like eye strain, neck pain, and posture problems.

Encouraging a Balanced Lifestyle

Screen-free spaces help you reclaim balance in a world that often feels dominated by digital demands. They act as anchors, grounding you in what truly matters and providing a respite from the relentless pace of modern life.

- **Rediscovering Joy:** Simple, offline activities—like reading a book, baking, or enjoying a sunset—become sources of genuine happiness and fulfillment.

- **Setting Boundaries:** Establishing tech-free zones reinforces the importance of creating boundaries between digital and real life.

- **Reconnecting with Nature:** Outdoor, screen-free spaces, such as parks or gardens, can further enhance well-being by reducing stress and fostering a sense of calm.

Examples of Screen-Free Spaces

1. **The Dining Table:** A place for meals and meaningful conversations without the intrusion of devices.

2. **The Bedroom:** A sanctuary for rest, relaxation, and intimacy, free from blue light and digital distractions.

3. **The Living Room:** A zone for family bonding, creative hobbies, or quiet reading.

4. **Outdoor Areas:** Gardens, patios, or nearby parks where you can reconnect with nature and enjoy physical activity.

5. **The Workspace:** A minimalist, screen-free corner for brainstorming, journaling, or working on offline projects

The Ripple Effect of Screen-Free Spaces

The benefits of physical spaces free from screens extend beyond the immediate moment. Over time, they:

- Foster healthier habits and routines.

- Enhance your ability to focus and prioritize tasks.

- Deepen your connections with yourself and others.

- Reduce dependency on technology and restore balance to your life.

Conclusion: The Freedom in Unplugging

The power of physical spaces free from screens lies in their ability to help you slow down, breathe deeply, and embrace life as it unfolds. These sanctuaries are reminders that the world beyond the screen is rich with possibilities for connection, creativity, and joy. By intentionally carving out screen-free spaces in your daily life, you take a vital step toward living with greater purpose and presence.

Tools and strategies to minimize distractions.

In a world filled with constant notifications, endless scrolling, and competing demands for attention, minimizing distractions is essential to regain focus and productivity. While it may feel overwhelming to fight the pull of digital interruptions, practical tools and strategies can help you reclaim control and create a more intentional, distraction-free environment.

1. Turn Off Non-Essential Notifications

Notifications are one of the biggest culprits in breaking focus. Each ping or vibration creates a psychological urge to check your device, pulling you away from what matters.

- **How to Manage Notifications:**
  - Disable notifications for non-essential apps like social media or games.
  - Set "Do Not Disturb" or "Focus" modes during work hours or personal time.
  - Use widgets or summaries that consolidate notifications to review them on your own schedule.

2. Use Productivity Apps and Tools

Technology can be part of the solution when used intentionally. A variety of apps and tools are designed to help you limit distractions and stay on task.

- **Recommended Tools:**
  - **Focus Apps:** Apps like Forest or Focus@Will help you stay concentrated by blocking distractions or providing ambient focus-enhancing sounds.
  - **Website Blockers:** Tools like Freedom, StayFocusd, or Cold Turkey block distracting websites during set hours.
  - **Time Management Apps:** Apps like Toggl or RescueTime track how you spend your time and help you identify productivity pitfalls.

3. Create a Dedicated Workspace

A clutter-free, organized workspace signals your brain that it's time to focus. Keep this space free of distractions to enhance productivity.

- **Workspace Tips:**
  - Remove unnecessary tech devices or gadgets that tempt you to multitask.
  - Use noise-canceling headphones or play focus music to drown out distractions.
  - Keep only tools relevant to your task, such as notebooks, pens, or your computer.

4. Adopt Time-Blocking Techniques

Time-blocking involves dividing your day into focused, distraction-free segments dedicated to specific tasks. This method helps you structure your time and maintain a clear sense of purpose.

- **How to Use Time-Blocking:**
  - Allocate specific blocks of time for high-priority tasks, breaks, and meetings.
  - Use tools like Google Calendar or apps like Notion to plan your time effectively.
  - Stick to the schedule and avoid switching tasks during a time block.

5. Establish Device-Free Zones

Designating certain areas as screen-free helps minimize distractions and encourages intentional engagement with tasks or people.

- **Examples of Device-Free Zones:**

- The dining table to focus on meals and conversations.

- The bedroom to improve sleep and relaxation.

- A reading nook for uninterrupted leisure or learning.

6. Limit Multitasking

Multitasking might feel productive, but it often reduces efficiency and focus. Instead, practice single-tasking by giving your full attention to one activity at a time.

- **Strategies to Stop Multitasking:**

  - Close unused tabs and apps while working.

  - Use the Pomodoro Technique: 25 minutes of focused work followed by a 5-minute break.

  - Write down tasks in order of priority and tackle them sequentially.

7. Set Clear Boundaries with Others

Sometimes, distractions come from the people around you. Setting clear expectations can help minimize interruptions.

- **How to Communicate Boundaries:**

  - Let coworkers or family know when you need uninterrupted focus time.

  - Use visual cues, like a "Do Not Disturb" sign, to indicate when you're busy.

  - Schedule dedicated times to connect with others so they know when you'll be available.

8. Practice Mindfulness

Distractions often stem from a restless mind. Mindfulness techniques can help you build awareness of your focus and redirect attention when it wanders.

- **Mindfulness Practices:**
  - Start your day with a 5-minute meditation to set the tone for focus.
  - Take short breaks to breathe deeply and reset your mind during work sessions.
  - Reflect on your productivity at the end of each day to identify areas for improvement.

9. Leverage Physical Tools

Sometimes, low-tech solutions are the most effective for minimizing distractions.

- **Useful Physical Tools:**
  - **Analog Timers:** Use a physical timer for time-blocking or the Pomodoro Technique.
  - **Notebooks:** Write down tasks and ideas to avoid reaching for your phone to "jot something down."
  - **Sticky Notes:** Place reminders or motivational messages in your workspace to keep you on track.

10. Develop a Digital Detox Routine

Regularly disconnecting from devices helps train your brain to focus on non-digital tasks.

- **Simple Detox Practices:**
  - Schedule tech-free hours each day to focus on offline activities.

- Turn off your phone during meals, walks, or creative sessions.
- Try a "no-tech evening" once a week to reset your mind.

11. Monitor and Adjust Regularly

Minimizing distractions isn't a one-time effort—it requires regular reflection and adjustment. Periodically assess what's working and refine your strategies as needed.

- **Reflection Tips:**
    - Review your productivity and identify recurring distractions.
    - Experiment with new tools or techniques to optimize your workflow.
    - Celebrate small wins, like completing a day with fewer interruptions.

Conclusion: Mastering Your Attention

The power to minimize distractions lies in intentional actions and consistent habits. By leveraging tools and strategies to limit interruptions, you can create an environment that supports focus, productivity, and peace of mind. Whether it's turning off notifications, establishing device-free zones, or practicing mindfulness, each small step brings you closer to a life where you control your attention—not the other way around.

Chapter 6: 7-Day Digital Reset Challenge

The 7-Day Digital Reset Challenge is designed to help you gradually unplug from technology, reclaim control over your digital habits, and experience the benefits of a more balanced lifestyle. Each day focuses on a specific aspect of digital detoxing, providing manageable steps and strategies to ease you into this transformative journey.

Day 1: Awareness and Assessment

The first step to any change is awareness. Spend the day observing and recording your digital habits without making any immediate changes.

- **Tasks for Day 1:**
    - Use a screen-time tracker (e.g., Screen Time for iOS or Digital Wellbeing for Android) to monitor your usage.
    - Write down how often you check your devices and which apps or platforms you spend the most time on.
    - Reflect on how you feel after using technology. Are you energized, drained, or indifferent?
- **Goal:** Identify the patterns and triggers that dominate your digital habits.

Day 2: Declutter Your Digital Environment

A cluttered digital space leads to unnecessary distractions. Dedicate Day 2 to cleaning up your devices and setting up tools to support your detox.

- **Tasks for Day 2:**

- Delete unused apps, subscriptions, or files.

- Organize your home screen by prioritizing essential apps and removing distractions (e.g., social media) to secondary screens.

- Turn off non-essential notifications to reduce interruptions.

- **Goal:** Create a streamlined, distraction-free digital environment.

Day 3: Establish Screen-Free Zones

Today, designate specific areas in your home or workspace where screens are not allowed.

- **Tasks for Day 3:**

  - Choose at least one space, such as the dining table or bedroom, to be screen-free.

  - Set up physical alternatives in these spaces, like books, board games, or puzzles.

  - Communicate these new boundaries to family or roommates to ensure they're respected.

- **Goal:** Begin reclaiming certain parts of your environment for offline activities.

Day 4: Practice Intentional Tech Use

Instead of mindless scrolling, use technology with purpose and set clear boundaries for its use.

- **Tasks for Day 4:**

  - Schedule specific times for checking emails, social media, or other platforms.

- Implement the Pomodoro Technique: 25 minutes of focused work followed by a 5-minute screen-free break.

- Replace one hour of screen time with a meaningful offline activity, like journaling, exercising, or cooking.

- **Goal:** Shift from reactive, habitual tech use to intentional engagement.

Day 5: Social Media Detox

Today, focus specifically on reducing or eliminating social media use.

- **Tasks for Day 5:**

  - Log out of social media apps or move them to a less accessible folder on your phone.

  - Replace your morning or evening scroll with a calming activity like meditation or reading.

  - Spend time connecting with someone in person instead of through a screen.

- **Goal:** Break the cycle of social media dependency and focus on meaningful interactions.

Day 6: Embrace Offline Experiences

Dedicate the day to exploring offline activities and enjoying the benefits of being unplugged.

- **Tasks for Day 6:**

  - Plan a tech-free outing, such as a hike, a visit to a museum, or a picnic in the park.

- Engage in a creative hobby, like painting, cooking, or writing.

  - Reflect on how these activities make you feel compared to digital consumption.

- **Goal:** Rediscover the joy of real-world experiences and the fulfillment they bring.

Day 7: Reflect and Plan for the Future

Congratulations! You've completed the challenge. Use this day to reflect on your experience and plan how to maintain the habits you've developed.

- **Tasks for Day 7:**

  - Journal about the changes you've noticed in your focus, mood, and overall well-being.

  - Identify which strategies worked best for you and how you can integrate them into your daily life.

  - Set long-term goals for ongoing digital detoxing, such as scheduling weekly screen-free days or monthly social media breaks.

- **Goal:** Solidify your commitment to a healthier, more intentional relationship with technology.

Conclusion: Your Path Forward

The 7-Day Digital Reset Challenge is a powerful starting point for breaking free from digital dependency and cultivating a balanced lifestyle. Each day builds on the last, providing you with practical tools and habits that can be sustained over time. As you move forward, remember that the journey doesn't end here—small, consistent efforts will help you maintain the benefits of your reset and continue thriving in a tech-saturated world.

Replacing screen time with meaningful activities.

One of the most effective ways to break free from excessive screen time is to fill those moments with meaningful, enriching activities. By intentionally replacing digital distractions with offline pursuits, you not only regain time but also enhance your overall well-being, foster creativity, and strengthen personal connections.

The Importance of Replacing Screen Time

Excessive screen use often fills idle moments with low-value activities, such as mindless scrolling or binge-watching. Replacing this time with meaningful activities allows you to:

- **Boost Mental and Physical Health:** Engaging in hobbies, exercise, or mindfulness practices improves focus, reduces stress, and promotes well-being.

- **Foster Deeper Connections:** Spending time with family, friends, or your community nurtures relationships and creates lasting memories.

- **Rediscover Joy and Fulfillment:** Hobbies and passions that align with your values bring genuine satisfaction, unlike the fleeting pleasure of digital distractions.

Meaningful Activities to Try

1. Nurture Creativity

Creativity flourishes in moments of stillness and focus. Replacing screen time with creative pursuits can spark inspiration and a sense of accomplishment.

- **Ideas:**

- Writing: Start a journal, write poetry, or work on a novel.

- Art: Explore drawing, painting, or crafting.

- Music: Learn a new instrument or compose your own songs.

- **Benefits:** Enhances problem-solving skills and provides an outlet for self-expression.

2. Engage in Physical Activities

Replacing sedentary screen time with movement improves your physical health and mental clarity.

- **Ideas:**

  - Take a walk in nature or explore a new hiking trail.

  - Join a fitness class, such as yoga, dance, or martial arts.

  - Try home workouts or practice mindfulness through stretching.

- **Benefits:** Boosts energy levels, improves mood, and promotes cardiovascular health.

3. Cultivate Mindfulness

Mindfulness practices help you reconnect with the present moment and reduce stress.

- **Ideas:**

  - Meditation: Use guided sessions or simply sit in quiet reflection.

- o Breathing Exercises: Practice deep breathing techniques to calm your mind.

- o Gratitude Journaling: Write down things you're grateful for each day.

- **Benefits:** Reduces anxiety, sharpens focus, and fosters emotional resilience.

4. Strengthen Relationships

Replace solitary screen time with shared experiences that build stronger bonds.

- **Ideas:**

   - o Family Time: Cook a meal together, play board games, or have a tech-free movie night.

   - o Socializing: Meet friends for coffee, plan a group outing, or host a game night.

   - o Volunteering: Join community service projects to make a positive impact.

- **Benefits:** Fosters connection, empathy, and a sense of belonging.

5. Explore New Skills and Hobbies

Learning something new is a productive and rewarding way to spend your time.

- **Ideas:**

   - o Take up gardening and grow your own plants or vegetables.

   - o Enroll in a class, such as cooking, photography, or pottery.

- Learn a new language or skill through books or in-person lessons.

- **Benefits:** Keeps your mind active and builds confidence.

6. Embrace Reading and Learning

Books and offline resources provide a wealth of knowledge and entertainment.

- **Ideas:**
  - Read fiction to escape into new worlds or non-fiction to expand your understanding of a topic.
  - Join a book club to share your reading experiences with others.
  - Listen to audiobooks or podcasts while engaging in a non-digital activity like walking or cleaning.

- **Benefits:** Enhances focus, broadens horizons, and stimulates intellectual growth.

7. Reconnect with Nature

Spending time outdoors helps you unplug and rejuvenate your mind and body.

- **Ideas:**
  - Go for a picnic, visit a local park, or spend time by the water.
  - Try birdwatching, stargazing, or simply sit and enjoy the fresh air.
  - Participate in outdoor sports, such as cycling or kayaking.

- **Benefits:** Reduces stress, boosts creativity, and improves physical health.

Tips for Replacing Screen Time Successfully

1. Start Small

Begin by replacing 15-30 minutes of screen time with a meaningful activity. Gradually increase this duration as it becomes a natural part of your routine.

2. Schedule Screen-Free Time

Block off specific times in your day for offline activities, such as during meals, evenings, or weekends. Treat these times as sacred.

3. Keep Alternatives Handy

Make meaningful activities easily accessible by keeping books, art supplies, or workout gear within reach. This reduces the temptation to default to screens.

4. Find Accountability Partners

Share your goals with family or friends and involve them in your screen-free activities. This makes the process more enjoyable and helps you stay committed.

5. Reflect on Your Progress

Regularly review how these activities make you feel compared to screen time. Celebrate the positive changes, such as increased energy, focus, or joy.

Conclusion: The Rewards of Meaningful Activities

Replacing screen time with meaningful activities is not just about filling the hours—it's about creating a life enriched with purpose, joy, and connection. By engaging in pursuits that align with your values and interests, you can transform idle scrolling into moments of fulfillment and growth. The more you invest in these meaningful alternatives, the less you'll miss the screens.

Tracking your progress and reflecting on changes.

Embarking on a digital detox journey is a meaningful step toward a healthier, more intentional lifestyle. However, to make lasting changes, it's essential to track your progress and reflect on the impact of your efforts. Regular self-assessment not only keeps you motivated but also provides valuable insights into what works and what needs adjustment.

The Importance of Tracking Your Progress

Tracking your progress allows you to:

- **Measure Success:** See tangible improvements in your habits, focus, and overall well-being.

- **Stay Accountable:** Consistent monitoring reinforces commitment to your goals.

- **Identify Patterns:** Recognize triggers or times when you're most tempted to return to old habits.

- **Celebrate Wins:** Acknowledge milestones, no matter how small, to keep your momentum.

How to Track Your Progress

1. Use a Journal or Tracker

Keeping a written or digital record of your detox journey helps you stay organized and focused.

- **What to Record:**
  - Daily screen time (use tools like Screen Time for iOS or Digital Wellbeing for Android).

- Activities you replaced screen time with and how they made you feel.

- Challenges you faced and how you addressed them.

- Reflections on your mood, energy levels, and productivity.

- **Example Journal Entry:**

  - **Date:** November 23

  - **Screen Time:** Reduced from 5 hours to 3 hours.

  - **Replacements:** Read for 30 minutes, went for a walk, cooked dinner.

  - **Reflections:** Felt more present and relaxed. Struggled with the urge to check social media after dinner.

2. Use Apps for Automated Tracking

Leverage technology to monitor your digital habits automatically.

- **Recommended Apps:**

  - **RescueTime:** Tracks time spent on apps and websites and provides productivity insights.

  - **Moment:** Helps monitor screen time and set goals for reduction.

  - **Habitica:** Turns habit-tracking into a game, making it fun and engaging.

3. Create Visual Progress Charts

Seeing your progress visually can be incredibly motivating. Use graphs, charts, or even stickers on a calendar to represent your achievements.

- **Ideas for Visual Tracking:**
  - A bar graph showing daily reductions in screen time.
  - A calendar where each screen-free day is marked with a sticker.
  - A pie chart dividing time spent on meaningful activities versus screen time.

Reflecting on Changes

Reflection is key to understanding the deeper impact of your detox efforts. Set aside time regularly to evaluate how your digital habits and lifestyle have evolved.

1. Ask Yourself Reflective Questions

Use these prompts to guide your reflections:

- **Behavioral Changes:** How have your digital habits shifted since starting the detox?
- **Emotional Impact:** How do you feel during screen-free moments compared to before?
- **Productivity Gains:** Have you noticed improvements in focus, efficiency, or creativity?
- **Relationships:** Have your interactions with family, friends, or colleagues improved?
- **Challenges:** What temptations or obstacles are still present, and how can you address them?

2. Compare Before and After

Revisit your initial goals and observations to see how far you've come.

- **Before Detox:**
    - Spent an average of 6 hours on screens daily.
    - Felt anxious without checking notifications.
    - Neglected hobbies like painting or reading.
- **After Detox:**
    - Reduced screen time to 3 hours daily.
    - Feel calmer and less reactive to notifications.
    - Rediscovered joy in painting and finished two books.

3. Write Down Lessons Learned

Capture insights and lessons to guide your future digital habits.

- **Examples of Lessons:**
    - "I'm most tempted to scroll social media when I'm bored—having a book nearby helps."
    - "Screen-free mornings improve my focus and set a positive tone for the day."
    - "Taking a walk instead of watching videos clears my mind and boosts my energy."

Celebrating Progress

Acknowledging and celebrating your achievements, no matter how small, reinforces positive habits and keeps you motivated.

- **Ways to Celebrate:**
  - Treat yourself to something meaningful, like a new book or a special outing.
  - Share your progress with a friend or accountability partner for encouragement.
  - Reflect on how far you've come and set new goals to build on your success.

Adjusting Your Approach

As you reflect, you may discover areas where you can refine your strategy.

1. Identify What Works Best

Note which activities, tools, or techniques were most effective in reducing screen time and improving your well-being.

2. Tackle Persistent Challenges

If certain distractions remain, brainstorm new ways to address them. For example:

- **Challenge:** Struggling to stay offline during breaks.
- **Solution:** Prepare a list of quick, offline activities, like stretching, journaling, or sipping tea mindfully.

3. Set New Goals

As you grow more comfortable with reduced screen time, set fresh objectives to deepen your digital detox journey.

- **Examples of New Goals:**
  - Limit screen time to 2 hours daily.

- Dedicate one entire weekend per month to being offline.

- Replace an hour of social media scrolling with a fitness class or volunteering.

Conclusion: Your Path to Lasting Change

Tracking your progress and reflecting on changes transforms a temporary detox into a sustainable lifestyle shift. By regularly evaluating your journey, celebrating your achievements, and adjusting your approach, you can continue to build a healthier, more intentional relationship with technology. Each step forward reinforces the power of living with presence and purpose, both on and off the screen.

Chapter 7: Mindful Digital Consumption

Embracing Intentionality in Your Tech Use

In a world of endless notifications, infinite scrolling, and algorithm-driven feeds, technology can either enrich your life or overwhelm it. Mindful digital consumption is about embracing intentionality—making deliberate choices about how, when, and why you use technology. By shifting from passive engagement to purposeful interaction, you can take control of your digital habits and foster a healthier relationship with your devices.

The Principles of Mindful Digital Consumption

Mindful consumption involves aligning your tech use with your values, priorities, and goals. The following principles lay the foundation for intentional engagement:

1. **Awareness:** Understand how and why you use technology, identifying both productive and unproductive patterns.

2. **Purpose:** Use devices with a clear intention, rather than as a default response to boredom or habit.

3. **Balance:** Prioritize offline activities and set boundaries to ensure technology supports, rather than detracts from, your well-being.

Steps to Embrace Intentional Tech Use

1. Define Your Tech Values and Goals

Start by reflecting on what role technology should play in your life. Ask yourself:

- What activities or platforms genuinely add value to my life?

- Which habits or apps feel like time-wasters or sources of stress?

- How can I use technology to align with my personal and professional goals?

- **Example Goals:**

  o Use social media for professional networking rather than mindless scrolling.

  o Spend less time on entertainment apps and more on learning new skills or hobbies.

2. Audit Your Digital Habits

Conduct a self-assessment to identify areas for improvement.

- Track your screen time and app usage using built-in tools like Screen Time (iOS) or Digital Wellbeing (Android).

- Note when and why you reach for your device. Are you seeking connection, avoiding discomfort, or simply acting out of habit?

- **Reflection Questions:**

  o Which apps or activities consume the most time?

  o How do I feel after using certain platforms—energized, drained, or indifferent?

3. Set Clear Intentions for Tech Use

Before engaging with your device, pause and ask yourself:

- What is my purpose in using this app or platform right now?

- How long do I plan to spend on this activity?

By setting intentions, you can avoid falling into the trap of mindless consumption and focus on meaningful interactions.

- **Example Intentions:**
  - Check emails for 15 minutes to respond to urgent messages.
  - Use Instagram for 10 minutes to post an update or engage with friends.

4. Curate Your Digital Environment

A cluttered digital environment contributes to distraction and overwhelm. Simplify and optimize your tech space to encourage intentional use.

- **Tips for Digital Decluttering:**
  - Unfollow accounts or unsubscribe from newsletters that don't align with your goals or values.
  - Organize your home screen by keeping only essential apps visible.
  - Turn off non-essential notifications to reduce interruptions.

5. Schedule Screen Time with Purpose

Designate specific times for using technology and stick to them. This helps you create boundaries and prevents tech use from bleeding into every aspect of your day.

- **Examples:**
  - Check social media or news apps only during designated time blocks, such as a 30-minute break after lunch.

- Avoid using devices during meals, family time, or the first hour after waking up.

6. Practice the "Pause Before Engaging" Rule

Whenever you feel the urge to pick up your phone or open a new tab, pause and ask yourself:

- Is this action aligned with my intentions?

- Is there a better way to address my need or desire right now (e.g., boredom, curiosity, or stress)?

This simple habit trains your brain to act deliberately rather than reactively.

7. Replace Digital Habits with Offline Alternatives

Identify tech habits that feel unproductive or excessive, and replace them with fulfilling offline activities.

- **Examples:**
  - Replace evening social media scrolling with reading a book or journaling.
  - Use a physical notebook for task tracking instead of relying on an app.
  - Engage in face-to-face conversations instead of texting or emailing.

The Benefits of Mindful Digital Consumption

Embracing intentionality in your tech use offers numerous benefits that extend to all aspects of your life:

1. Enhanced Focus and Productivity

By eliminating mindless distractions, you create more time and mental clarity to dedicate to meaningful tasks.

2. Improved Emotional Well-Being

Mindful tech use reduces feelings of comparison, overwhelm, and anxiety that often stem from excessive or unintentional screen time.

3. Stronger Relationships

When you're fully present during interactions, you foster deeper connections with family, friends, and colleagues.

4. Greater Sense of Fulfillment

Intentional engagement with technology ensures that your digital activities contribute to your goals, passions, and growth, rather than detracting from them.

Reflecting on Your Progress

Regularly evaluate your digital habits to ensure you're staying aligned with your intentions. Ask yourself:

- Have I noticed changes in my focus, mood, or relationships?

- Are there new habits or tools I can adopt to further improve my tech use?

- What challenges have I faced, and how can I address them moving forward?

Conclusion: Living with Purpose in the Digital Age

Mindful digital consumption is about more than reducing screen time—it's about aligning your technology use with what truly matters to you. By embracing intentionality, you can transform your relationship with technology from one of passive reliance to one of purposeful engagement. The result is a life filled with clarity, balance, and meaningful connections—both online and offline.

Establishing clear boundaries: Time limits, app audits, and no-phone zones.

In the digital age, setting boundaries around technology use is essential for maintaining focus, balance, and well-being. Without clear limits, the constant presence of devices can blur the line between work and personal life, intrude on relationships, and erode mental clarity. Establishing thoughtful boundaries empowers you to regain control and prioritize what truly matters.

1. Setting Time Limits

Time limits help prevent excessive screen use and ensure that your digital habits align with your priorities. By defining how much time you spend on certain apps or devices, you can break the cycle of mindless scrolling and reclaim hours for more meaningful activities.

Steps to Implement Time Limits:

- **Track Current Usage:** Use tools like Screen Time (iOS) or Digital Wellbeing (Android) to monitor how much time you spend on apps daily.

- **Set Realistic Goals:** Based on your needs and lifestyle, decide on reasonable daily or weekly limits for specific apps or activities.

  - **Examples:** Limit social media to 30 minutes per day or video streaming to 2 hours on weekends.

- **Use Built-In Features:** Enable time-limit settings on your phone or third-party apps to enforce these boundaries. These tools can lock you out of apps once you reach your limit.

- **Create Time Blocks:** Designate specific times for tech use and stick to them. For example:

    o Check emails between 9 AM and 10 AM only.

    o Use social media during a 15-minute afternoon break.

2. Conducting App Audits

Not all apps serve your goals or well-being. An app audit allows you to identify which digital tools add value and which ones detract from your life. Regularly reviewing your app usage helps you curate a digital environment that supports your intentionality.

How to Perform an App Audit:

- **Categorize Your Apps:** Divide apps into categories like productivity, communication, entertainment, and essential tools.

- **Evaluate Each App:** Ask yourself:

    o Does this app add value to my life or simply waste my time?

    o How often do I use this app, and is it necessary?

    o Does this app make me feel good or leave me feeling drained?

- **Delete or Disable:** Remove apps that don't align with your priorities or that you use excessively. For instance:

- Uninstall games or social media apps that consume hours without providing meaningful benefits.

- Use browser-based versions of apps like Instagram to add friction and reduce compulsive use.

- **Organize Your Home Screen:** Keep only essential or frequently used apps on your home screen. Move less critical apps to folders or secondary screens to reduce temptation.

3. Creating No-Phone Zones

Designating certain areas as phone-free zones helps reinforce boundaries and encourages presence and mindfulness. These zones promote better relationships, focus, and relaxation by creating tech-free sanctuaries.

Examples of No-Phone Zones:

- **The Dining Table:** Encourage meaningful conversations during meals without the distraction of devices.

- **The Bedroom:** Improve sleep quality and intimacy by keeping phones out of the bedroom. Use a traditional alarm clock instead of your phone to wake up.

- **The Living Room:** Create a space for reading, hobbies, or family bonding without the interference of screens.

- **Workspaces:** Keep your desk free of unnecessary devices to enhance productivity and focus.

Tips for Enforcing No-Phone Zones:

- **Use Physical Barriers:** Create a designated spot, like a charging station in another room, where devices can be stored during phone-free times.

- **Communicate Rules:** Let family members or roommates know about the no-phone zones to ensure everyone respects the boundaries.

- **Incorporate Alternatives:** Provide offline activities, like board games or books, to fill the time usually spent on screens.

The Benefits of Clear Boundaries

1. **Increased Focus and Productivity:** Time limits and no-phone zones eliminate distractions, allowing you to concentrate on tasks and complete them efficiently.

2. **Enhanced Relationships:** Removing screens during meals or family time fosters deeper connections and meaningful conversations.

3. **Better Mental Health:** App audits help reduce exposure to toxic or draining digital content, promoting a more positive mindset.

4. **Improved Sleep Quality:** Keeping phones out of the bedroom minimizes blue light exposure and prevents late-night scrolling.

5. **Greater Sense of Balance:** Setting boundaries creates space for hobbies, relaxation, and personal growth, helping you live with intention.

Maintaining Your Boundaries

Setting boundaries is one thing, but sticking to them requires consistency and commitment.

Tips to Stay on Track:

- **Reflect Regularly:** Periodically evaluate how well your boundaries are working and adjust them if necessary.

- **Reward Yourself:** Celebrate milestones, like completing a week with reduced screen time, to stay motivated.

- **Enlist Support:** Share your boundaries with family or friends and ask them to hold you accountable.

- **Be Flexible:** Allow for exceptions when necessary, but ensure they don't become habits.

Conclusion: Taking Back Control

Establishing clear boundaries through time limits, app audits, and no-phone zones empowers you to use technology intentionally rather than letting it control you. By creating space for meaningful interactions, focused work, and restful moments, you can foster a balanced, fulfilling lifestyle in a tech-saturated world. Remember, boundaries are not about restriction—they're about protecting what matters most.

Learning to curate your online experience for positivity.

The online world has the potential to enrich your life, offering knowledge, connections, and inspiration. However, without intentional curation, it can also overwhelm you with negativity, distractions, and stress. By curating your digital spaces, you take control of what you see, engage with, and absorb—turning your online experience into a source of positivity and growth.

The Power of Intentional Curation

Your digital environment impacts your mindset, emotions, and daily interactions. A curated online experience can:

- **Reduce Stress:** Minimize exposure to toxic content and information overload.

- **Boost Inspiration:** Fill your feed with uplifting and motivational content.

- **Foster Growth:** Focus on platforms, communities, and content that align with your values and goals.

- **Improve Mental Health:** Create a virtual space that encourages self-reflection, gratitude, and joy.

Steps to Curate a Positive Online Experience

1. Audit Your Online Environment

The first step to curating positivity is understanding what currently dominates your digital landscape.

- **How to Audit:**

    o Review your social media feeds, email subscriptions, and frequently visited websites.

    o Ask yourself:

        ▪ Does this content make me feel inspired or drained?

        ▪ Does this person, page, or platform align with my values?

        ▪ Am I gaining meaningful insights or wasting time here?

2. Follow Accounts That Inspire and Uplift

Surround yourself with content that adds value to your life. Choose creators, organizations, and communities that align with your passions and priorities.

- **Examples of Positive Content:**
    - Inspirational speakers, coaches, or thought leaders.
    - Accounts focused on personal growth, mental health, or creativity.
    - Platforms sharing educational or skill-building content.
    - Niche communities that share your hobbies or interests (e.g., art, fitness, or gardening).

3. Unfollow or Mute Negative Influences

Not all content you encounter will contribute to a positive mindset. Decluttering your digital space is essential to reduce negativity.

- **Who to Unfollow or Mute:**
    - Accounts that promote drama, toxicity, or divisiveness.
    - Pages that make you feel inadequate, anxious, or pressured to compare.
    - Sources of misinformation or sensationalized news.

- **Tip:** Use platform features like muting or unfollowing to adjust your feed without completely severing connections if it feels uncomfortable.

4. Limit Exposure to News and Overwhelming Information

While staying informed is important, constant exposure to negative news can take a toll on your mental health.

- **Strategies to Manage News Consumption:**
    - Set specific times to check the news rather than engaging throughout the day.
    - Follow reliable, balanced news outlets to avoid sensationalism.
    - Focus on solutions-oriented content that highlights positive developments.

5. Engage Actively, Not Passively

Scrolling mindlessly through endless feeds can leave you feeling disconnected and unfulfilled. Shift from passive consumption to active engagement.

- **How to Engage Positively:**
    - Comment thoughtfully on posts that resonate with you.
    - Share content that inspires or helps others.
    - Participate in meaningful online discussions or forums.

6. Diversify Your Digital Diet

Avoid echo chambers by exploring different perspectives and broadening the type of content you consume. This fosters curiosity and balanced thinking.

- **Examples of Diversification:**
    - Follow creators from diverse backgrounds or fields of expertise.
    - Explore content in areas you're curious about, such as science, history, or art.

- Join online groups or communities that promote constructive dialogue and learning.

7. Set Boundaries for Online Interactions

Not every interaction online will be positive. Setting boundaries protects your energy and peace of mind.

- **Tips for Healthy Interactions:**
  - Avoid engaging with trolls or negative comments; instead, focus on constructive exchanges.
  - Set limits on responding to messages or emails to prevent burnout.
  - Leave groups or conversations that no longer serve your growth or well-being.

8. Use Algorithms to Your Advantage

Algorithms shape much of your online experience. By intentionally interacting with positive content, you can train these algorithms to show you more of what uplifts you.

- **How to Train Algorithms:**
  - Like, share, and comment on posts that align with your interests and values.
  - Avoid clicking on or engaging with clickbait or toxic content.
  - Use platform tools to hide or block irrelevant or negative posts.

9. Balance Online Time with Offline Activities

Even the most positive online experience can't replace the benefits of real-world interactions and activities. Balance is key.

- **Suggestions for Offline Balance:**
  - Dedicate time to hobbies, exercise, or face-to-face conversations.
  - Implement screen-free hours or zones in your daily routine.
  - Practice mindfulness or gratitude journaling to stay grounded.

Benefits of a Curated Online Experience

By intentionally shaping your digital spaces, you can:

- **Feel Empowered:** Engage with content that fuels your passions and goals.
- **Foster Connection:** Build relationships with like-minded people and communities.
- **Enhance Emotional Well-Being:** Reduce stress and negativity while boosting positivity and gratitude.
- **Reclaim Time:** Spend less time on unproductive scrolling and more on meaningful activities.

Reflect and Refine Regularly

Your needs and priorities evolve, and so should your online environment. Periodically assess your digital spaces to ensure they continue to serve your goals and values.

- **Reflection Prompts:**
  - What content or interactions bring me the most joy?

- Are there any new accounts or platforms that align with my current interests?

- How can I further reduce negativity in my digital spaces?

Conclusion: A Positive Digital Life

Curating your online experience for positivity is a powerful way to take control of your digital life. By intentionally choosing what you engage with, you can transform your feeds from sources of stress to spaces of inspiration and growth. Remember, the goal isn't to disconnect entirely—it's to connect meaningfully and intentionally with what truly uplifts you.

Chapter 8: The Role of Social Media in Modern Life

Weighing the Pros and Cons of Social Platforms

Social media has become an integral part of modern life, transforming the way we communicate, connect, and consume information. While it offers numerous benefits, it also comes with its fair share of challenges. By examining both the positive and negative aspects, we can better understand the role of social platforms in our lives and how to use them intentionally.

The Pros of Social Media

1. Enhanced Connectivity

Social media bridges geographical gaps, allowing people to stay connected regardless of distance.

- **Benefits:**
    - Instant communication with friends, family, and colleagues worldwide.
    - Strengthened relationships through shared updates, photos, and messages.
    - Opportunities to reconnect with old friends and expand social networks.

2. Access to Information and Resources

Social platforms serve as hubs for learning, sharing knowledge, and staying informed.

- **Benefits:**
    - Real-time news updates and information on global events.

- Access to educational content, tutorials, and expert advice.
- Platforms for spreading awareness about important causes and social issues.

3. Opportunities for Self-Expression

Social media provides a creative outlet for people to share their thoughts, talents, and passions.

- **Benefits:**
  - Platforms to showcase art, writing, music, or photography.
  - Spaces for sharing personal stories and inspiring others.
  - Tools to build personal brands and establish online identities.

4. Building Communities

Social platforms foster a sense of belonging by connecting people with shared interests.

- **Benefits:**
  - Online groups and forums for niche hobbies, causes, and professions.
  - Support networks for individuals facing similar challenges or goals.
  - Collaborative opportunities for like-minded individuals and organizations.

5. Business and Career Growth

For professionals and entrepreneurs, social media offers powerful tools for networking and promotion.

- **Benefits:**
    - Platforms for marketing products and services to a global audience.
    - Networking opportunities with industry leaders and potential clients.
    - Access to job postings, career advice, and professional development resources.

The Cons of Social Media

1. Addiction and Overuse

The design of social media platforms encourages prolonged and habitual use.

- **Challenges:**
    - Loss of productivity due to endless scrolling and distractions.
    - Increased screen time, leading to physical and mental fatigue.
    - Difficulty setting boundaries between online and offline life.

2. Mental Health Impacts

Excessive use of social media can negatively affect emotional well-being.

- **Challenges:**
    - Feelings of inadequacy due to curated highlight reels of others' lives.

- Anxiety or depression from cyberbullying or negative interactions.

- Stress from constant notifications and the fear of missing out (FOMO).

3. Spread of Misinformation

Social platforms can amplify false information, creating confusion and mistrust.

- **Challenges:**

    - Difficulty discerning credible sources from unreliable ones.

    - Viral spread of rumors, conspiracy theories, and fake news.

    - Polarization of opinions due to algorithm-driven echo chambers.

4. Privacy Concerns

Sharing personal information online poses risks to security and privacy.

- **Challenges:**

    - Unauthorized use of data by third parties or malicious actors.

    - Increased vulnerability to identity theft, hacking, or scams.

    - Lack of control over how platforms use or share user information.

5. Impact on Relationships

While social media can connect people, it can also strain real-world interactions.

- **Challenges:**
    - "Phubbing" (phone snubbing), where screen time interferes with in-person relationships.
    - Superficial connections that lack depth and authenticity.
    - Miscommunications or conflicts arising from digital interactions.

Striking a Balance: Intentional Social Media Use

To maximize the benefits of social media while minimizing its drawbacks, it's essential to approach it with intentionality.

1. Set Clear Goals for Use

Define the purpose of your social media engagement.

- **Examples:** Networking for professional growth, staying informed, or sharing creative work.

2. Limit Screen Time

Use time-management tools or set personal limits to prevent overuse.

- **Examples:**
    - Schedule specific times to check social platforms.
    - Use apps to track and reduce screen time.

3. Curate Your Feed

Follow accounts and pages that inspire, educate, or align with your values.

- **Tips:**
    - Unfollow negative influences or sources of stress.
    - Seek diverse perspectives to avoid echo chambers.

4. Prioritize Privacy

Take steps to protect your personal information.

- **Tips:**
    - Adjust privacy settings on your accounts.
    - Avoid sharing sensitive details publicly.

5. Balance Online and Offline Life

Ensure that social media enhances rather than replaces real-world experiences.

- **Tips:**
    - Designate screen-free times or zones in your day.
    - Invest in face-to-face interactions and offline activities.

Reflecting on Your Relationship with Social Media

Regularly evaluate the role of social platforms in your life. Ask yourself:

- Does my social media use align with my personal and professional goals?
- How does social media affect my mood, productivity, and relationships?
- What changes can I make to foster a healthier relationship with these platforms?

Conclusion: Navigating Social Media with Intention

Social media is neither inherently good nor bad—it's a tool whose impact depends on how you use it. By recognizing its benefits and challenges, you can create a balanced approach that leverages social platforms to enrich your life while protecting your mental health and well-being. Remember, you have the power to shape your online experience and ensure it serves your highest priorities.

Detox strategies tailored for social media.

Social media can be a powerful tool for connection and creativity, but it can also become overwhelming, consuming valuable time and negatively impacting mental health. A tailored social media detox helps you regain balance by intentionally limiting your usage, reducing distractions, and fostering a healthier relationship with these platforms. Whether you're looking for a temporary break or a long-term reset, these strategies can guide you toward mindful and intentional social media use.

1. Set Clear Goals for Your Detox

Define why you want to detox from social media and what you hope to achieve. This clarity will keep you motivated and help you focus on meaningful changes.

- **Questions to Ask Yourself:**
  - Am I spending too much time scrolling instead of pursuing other goals?
  - Does social media negatively affect my mood or self-esteem?
  - Do I want to be more present with loved ones or improve my productivity?

- **Example Goals:**
  - Reduce daily social media use to 30 minutes.
  - Eliminate evening scrolling to improve sleep.
  - Take a week-long break to focus on offline hobbies.

2. Gradually Reduce Usage

Instead of quitting social media cold turkey, gradually decrease your time on these platforms to make the transition smoother.

- **Steps to Reduce Usage:**
  - Use apps like Screen Time (iOS) or Digital Wellbeing (Android) to monitor and limit your daily screen time.
  - Set specific times for social media, such as 15 minutes in the morning and 15 minutes in the evening.
  - Replace one scrolling session per day with a productive or relaxing offline activity.

3. Turn Off Notifications

Notifications are designed to grab your attention and keep you coming back. Turning them off can reduce interruptions and help you focus on other tasks.

- **How to Manage Notifications:**
  - Disable notifications for all social media apps in your phone settings.
  - Use "Do Not Disturb" or "Focus" modes during work, meals, or family time.

- Keep app badges (those little red dots) hidden to avoid feeling compelled to check for updates.

4. Curate Your Feed

A detox isn't just about reducing time spent on social media—it's also about improving the quality of your online experience. Curating your feed ensures that what you see is inspiring, positive, and relevant to your goals.

- **Steps to Curate Your Feed:**
    - Unfollow or mute accounts that trigger stress, comparison, or negativity.
    - Follow creators and communities that align with your values and interests.
    - Avoid consuming content that promotes misinformation or divisive topics.

5. Create Screen-Free Zones and Times

Designate specific areas or periods in your day as social-media-free to reinforce boundaries.

- **Ideas for Screen-Free Zones:**
    - The dining table, to focus on mindful eating and meaningful conversations.
    - The bedroom, to improve sleep quality and relaxation.
    - Workspaces, to enhance focus and productivity.

- **Ideas for Screen-Free Times:**
    - The first hour after waking up, to start your day mindfully.

- The last hour before bed, to unwind and prepare for restful sleep.

- During family gatherings or social outings, to prioritize face-to-face connections.

6. Take a Temporary Break

A short-term detox, such as a weekend or week-long break, can help you reset your habits and evaluate your relationship with social media.

- **How to Take a Break:**

  - Announce your detox to friends and followers if you feel comfortable.

  - Log out of all social media accounts on your devices.

  - Delete apps temporarily to reduce temptation.

  - Plan offline activities to fill the time you'd usually spend scrolling.

7. Establish New Habits

A detox is an opportunity to replace social media habits with activities that enrich your life.

- **Suggestions for New Habits:**

  - **Morning Routine:** Replace checking social media with journaling, stretching, or reading.

  - **Downtime Activities:** Use breaks for meditation, a walk, or creative hobbies instead of scrolling.

  - **Evening Wind-Down:** Read a book, practice gratitude, or spend quality time with loved ones.

8. Use Alternative Tools to Stay Connected

If you're concerned about losing touch with friends or missing important updates, use alternative methods to stay connected.

- **Alternatives to Social Media:**
    - Text or call friends directly to maintain relationships.
    - Use email or group messaging apps for updates and coordination.
    - Attend in-person events or meetups to foster deeper connections.

9. Reflect on Your Progress

As you detox, take time to evaluate how your reduced social media use affects your mood, productivity, and overall well-being.

- **Reflection Questions:**
    - How do I feel during screen-free moments compared to before?
    - What offline activities bring me joy or fulfillment?
    - Do I notice improvements in my focus, energy, or relationships?

10. Set Long-Term Boundaries

After completing your detox, create sustainable boundaries to maintain a healthier relationship with social media.

- **Examples of Long-Term Boundaries:**
    - Limit social media use to specific times or days (e.g., no social media on Sundays).

- Keep your total daily screen time under one hour.
- Regularly audit and update your feed to ensure it remains positive and relevant.

The Benefits of a Social Media Detox

By detoxing from social media, you can experience a range of benefits:

- **Improved Mental Health:** Reduced anxiety, stress, and feelings of inadequacy.

- **Enhanced Focus:** More time and energy for meaningful tasks and goals.

- **Stronger Relationships:** Deeper connections with friends and family through face-to-face interactions.

- **Increased Creativity:** More time to explore hobbies and develop new skills.

- **Greater Self-Awareness:** A clearer understanding of your digital habits and priorities.

Conclusion: Mindful Social Media Use for a Balanced Life

A tailored social media detox is a powerful step toward creating a more intentional and balanced digital life. By implementing these strategies, you can break free from the constant pull of social platforms, focus on what truly matters, and cultivate a healthier, more positive relationship with technology. Remember, the goal isn't to eliminate social media—it's to use it in ways that enrich and uplift your life.

Finding joy in offline social connections.

In a world dominated by digital interactions, the joy of offline social connections is often overlooked. Yet, face-to-face interactions bring a depth and authenticity that no online platform can replicate. They foster genuine emotional bonds, enhance mental well-being, and remind us of the beauty of shared human experiences. Rediscovering joy in offline connections is not only fulfilling but also essential for a balanced and enriched life.

The Unique Power of Offline Connections

Offline interactions provide a sensory and emotional richness that goes beyond words or emojis.

- **Non-Verbal Communication:** Facial expressions, tone of voice, and body language deepen understanding and empathy.

- **Shared Experiences:** Activities like sharing a meal, laughing together, or enjoying a hike create lasting memories.

- **Genuine Presence:** Being physically present with others fosters trust, connection, and a sense of belonging.

The Benefits of Offline Social Connections

1. Improved Emotional Well-Being

Engaging with others in person boosts mood and reduces feelings of loneliness or isolation.

- **Why It Matters:**
  - Physical touch, like a hug or handshake, releases oxytocin, enhancing feelings of trust and happiness.
  - Face-to-face interactions lower stress levels by promoting relaxation and reducing cortisol production.

2. Stronger Relationships

Offline interactions deepen bonds and allow for more meaningful conversations.

- **Why It Matters:**
  - Uninterrupted time together builds intimacy and strengthens connections.
  - Real-world experiences create a foundation for trust and mutual understanding.

3. Increased Focus and Presence

Without the distractions of screens, you can fully engage with those around you.

- **Why It Matters:**
  - Being present shows others that you value their time and attention.
  - Focused interactions foster a sense of respect and appreciation.

Ways to Foster Offline Connections

1. Plan Regular Meetups

Prioritize time to connect with friends, family, or colleagues in person.

- **Ideas for Meetups:**
  - Host a potluck dinner or picnic.
  - Organize a game night with board games or card games.
  - Go for coffee or a casual walk to catch up.

2. Engage in Shared Activities

Doing something together strengthens bonds and makes interactions more dynamic.

- **Activity Suggestions:**
  - Take a fitness class, like yoga or dance, with a friend.
  - Join a local club or volunteer group to meet like-minded people.
  - Attend community events, such as farmers' markets or art shows.

3. Make Meals a Social Experience

Sharing food has always been a cornerstone of human connection.

- **How to Make it Meaningful:**
  - Cook a meal together, sharing recipes and techniques.
  - Host a family dinner with a no-phone policy to encourage conversation.
  - Explore new cuisines at local restaurants with friends or family.

4. Create Screen-Free Zones

Designate areas or times in your home for uninterrupted socializing.

- **Ideas for Screen-Free Spaces:**
  - The dining table during meals.

- The living room during family gatherings.

- Outdoor spaces like gardens or patios.

5. Celebrate Milestones Together

Marking important moments with others strengthens relationships and creates joyful memories.

- **Ideas for Celebrations:**

  - Host a small party for birthdays or anniversaries.

  - Celebrate achievements, like promotions or graduations, with a group outing.

  - Organize seasonal traditions, like holiday baking or summer barbecues.

Overcoming Barriers to Offline Connections

Sometimes, life's demands or social habits make it difficult to prioritize offline interactions. Here's how to overcome common challenges:

1. Busy Schedules

- **Solution:** Schedule social activities in advance and treat them as non-negotiable commitments.

- **Tip:** Combine socializing with daily tasks, like grocery shopping with a friend or exercising together.

2. Social Anxiety

- **Solution:** Start small with one-on-one interactions in low-pressure settings.

- **Tip:** Focus on shared activities, which take the pressure off constant conversation.

3. Digital Habits

- **Solution:** Set limits on screen time and intentionally replace it with in-person interactions.

- **Tip:** Use reminders or accountability partners to stick to your goals.

Rediscovering Joy in Offline Moments

1. Savor the Simplicity

Offline connections often thrive on simple, everyday joys:

- A heartfelt conversation over tea.

- A walk through a park, enjoying nature together.

- Sharing laughter over a funny story or memory.

2. Embrace Spontaneity

Some of the best moments come from unplanned interactions:

- Bumping into a friend and catching up on the spot.

- Inviting a neighbor over for an impromptu chat.

- Joining a friend for a last-minute adventure.

3. Reflect on Your Gratitude

After spending time offline with others, take a moment to reflect on the experience:

- What made the interaction special?

- How did it make you feel?

- What can you do to foster more moments like this?

The Lasting Impact of Offline Connections

Offline social interactions aren't just about enjoying the moment—they build a foundation for resilience, trust, and emotional fulfillment. They remind us of the value of human connection and the irreplaceable warmth of being present with others.

Conclusion: The Joy of Being Present

Finding joy in offline social connections is a powerful antidote to the isolation of the digital age. By prioritizing face-to-face interactions, you create meaningful relationships, foster emotional well-being, and enrich your life in ways no screen can replicate. Remember, the most valuable moments are often shared in the company of others, away from the glow of technology. Reconnect, be present, and savor the beauty of real-world connections.

Chapter 9: Tech for Good Tools and apps that help manage screen time effectively.

Tools and Apps That Help Manage Screen Time Effectively

Technology is often seen as the cause of screen-time overuse, but it can also be part of the solution. With the right tools and apps, you can monitor, reduce, and optimize your screen time, fostering a healthier digital balance. This chapter explores innovative ways technology can be leveraged for good, helping you take control of your habits while still reaping the benefits of the digital world.

The Role of Technology in Managing Screen Time

While technology itself can be addictive, it also provides powerful solutions for creating awareness and building healthier habits. Apps and tools designed for screen-time management offer features like:

- **Monitoring Usage:** Gain insights into how much time you spend on devices and specific apps.

- **Setting Limits:** Define boundaries to prevent overuse and encourage mindfulness.

- **Blocking Distractions:** Eliminate access to apps or websites during focus periods.

- **Encouraging Breaks:** Remind you to step away from screens and engage in offline activities.

By integrating these tools into your daily routine, you can take a proactive approach to digital detoxing without feeling overwhelmed.

Top Tools and Apps for Screen Time Management

1. Built-In Device Features

Most smartphones and computers come with built-in tools to track and limit screen time.

- **Screen Time (iOS):**

  - Tracks daily and weekly usage across apps and categories.

  - Allows you to set app limits, downtime schedules, and content restrictions.

  - Provides insights into your most-used apps and how often you pick up your device.

- **Digital Wellbeing (Android):**

  - Monitors app usage, notifications, and screen unlocks.

  - Offers focus modes to silence distracting apps during work or relaxation.

  - Includes bedtime mode to reduce blue light and remind you to wind down.

- **Focus Assist (Windows) & Screen Time (Mac):**

  - Built-in features for managing notifications and minimizing distractions during work.

2. Dedicated Screen Time Management Apps

If you need more advanced features or a cross-platform solution, these apps can help:

- **RescueTime:**

  - Tracks time spent on apps and websites, categorizing them as productive or unproductive.

- Provides detailed reports to identify patterns and areas for improvement.
- Includes a "FocusTime" feature that blocks distractions during work sessions.

- **Moment:**
  - Helps you set daily screen-time goals and tracks your progress.
  - Includes coaching features to guide you toward healthier habits.
  - Encourages "phone-free time" with notifications and challenges.

- **StayFocusd:**
  - A browser extension that limits time on distracting websites.
  - Allows you to block entire websites, specific pages, or even features like videos.
  - Ideal for maintaining focus during work or study sessions.

3. Apps for Blocking Distractions

For those who struggle with staying focused, these tools can help eliminate digital interruptions:

- **Freedom:**
  - Blocks distracting websites, apps, and even the entire internet if needed.
  - Works across multiple devices, including phones, tablets, and computers.

- Allows you to create custom blocklists and schedules.

- **Forest:**
  - Encourages you to stay off your phone by growing virtual trees while you focus.
  - Exiting the app before the timer ends "kills" the tree, reinforcing discipline.
  - Gamifies focus and allows you to earn rewards for planting real trees.

- **Cold Turkey:**
  - Offers powerful blocking features for apps, websites, and notifications.
  - Includes a "Scheduled Lock" feature to enforce focus times.
  - Allows you to set unbreakable blocks for maximum productivity.

4. Apps for Encouraging Breaks

Taking regular breaks from screens is essential for mental and physical well-being.

- **Stretchly:**
  - Reminds you to take breaks with customizable notifications.
  - Suggests quick stretching or mindfulness exercises during breaks.
  - Helps prevent eye strain and physical fatigue from prolonged screen use.

- **TimeOut:**
  - A macOS app that encourages micro-breaks and longer pauses throughout the day.
  - Displays soothing animations during breaks to help you relax.
  - Fully customizable for work and personal routines.
- **BreakFree:**
  - Tracks screen time and sends reminders to take regular breaks.
  - Includes tools to measure app usage and set goals for reducing overuse.

5. Family-Friendly Screen Time Solutions

For households with multiple users, especially children, these apps can help manage collective screen time:

- **Qustodio:**
  - Monitors and controls screen time for all devices in the family.
  - Allows parents to set limits, block apps, and view activity reports.
  - Provides location tracking and alerts for extra safety.
- **OurPact:**
  - Offers customizable screen-time schedules for kids.

- Lets parents remotely block or allow access to apps and websites.

- Includes a "Family Locator" feature for added peace of mind.

- **Google Family Link:**

  - Helps parents set app limits and approve downloads for children.

  - Tracks kids' device usage and suggests healthy tech habits.

  - Works seamlessly with Android and ChromeOS devices.

Integrating Tech for Good Into Your Routine

To maximize the benefits of these tools, incorporate them thoughtfully into your daily life:

1. Start Small and Build Habits

Begin with a single app or feature, like setting app limits or enabling focus mode, and gradually expand as you adapt to the changes.

2. Pair Tools with Intentional Practices

Combine apps with strategies like no-phone zones, scheduled breaks, or replacing screen time with offline activities.

3. Reflect and Adjust Regularly

Periodically review your progress and adjust settings or goals based on your needs. Use insights from tracking tools to refine your approach.

The Benefits of Using Tech to Manage Screen Time

When used effectively, screen-time management tools can help you:

- **Enhance Productivity:** Eliminate distractions and focus on meaningful tasks.

- **Improve Mental Health:** Reduce stress and overwhelm from excessive screen use.

- **Reclaim Time:** Free up hours for offline activities and personal growth.

- **Strengthen Relationships:** Prioritize face-to-face interactions over digital ones.

Conclusion: Harnessing Technology for Balance

Technology doesn't have to be the enemy of balance—it can be a powerful ally. By leveraging tools and apps designed to manage screen time, you can create healthier digital habits, achieve your goals, and enjoy the best of both the online and offline worlds. With intentional use, tech becomes a tool for good, helping you live a more mindful, focused, and fulfilling life.

Leveraging technology for productivity and personal growth.

Technology, when used intentionally, can be a catalyst for productivity and personal growth. From organizing tasks to learning new skills, the right tools and strategies can transform how you manage your time, achieve goals, and unlock your potential. This chapter explores how to harness the power of technology to work smarter, grow continuously, and lead a more fulfilling life.

The Dual Nature of Technology

While technology can be a source of distraction, it can also amplify your productivity and personal development. The key lies in intentional usage, where you focus on tools and practices that align with your goals. By leveraging technology wisely, you can:

- **Optimize Workflows:** Streamline tasks and save time for high-priority activities.

- **Enhance Learning:** Access resources to acquire new knowledge and skills.

- **Stay Organized:** Manage your time, goals, and responsibilities effectively.

- **Foster Growth:** Use apps and platforms to support your journey toward self-improvement.

1. Productivity Tools for Smarter Work

Task Management and Organization

Technology can help you keep track of tasks, deadlines, and projects with ease.

- **Tools to Try:**

    o **Todoist:** A versatile task manager for organizing daily to-do lists and long-term projects.

    o **Trello:** A visual project management tool that uses boards and cards to track progress.

    o **Notion:** A customizable workspace for managing tasks, notes, and collaborative projects.

- **How to Use:**

    o Break tasks into smaller, actionable steps.

- Set priorities and deadlines to stay on track.

- Integrate these tools with calendars or reminders for seamless scheduling.

Time Management and Focus

Technology can help you make the most of your time and eliminate distractions.

- **Tools to Try:**

  - **RescueTime:** Tracks how you spend your time online and identifies areas for improvement.

  - **Focus@Will:** Combines neuroscience-based music with productivity timers to enhance focus.

  - **Pomodoro Apps (e.g., Focus Booster):** Use the Pomodoro Technique to work in short, focused bursts.

- **How to Use:**

  - Schedule focused work sessions followed by short breaks.

  - Analyze time-tracking data to optimize your daily routines.

  - Use distraction-blocking features to maintain concentration.

2. Technology for Personal Growth

Lifelong Learning and Skill Development

Accessing high-quality educational resources has never been easier.

- **Platforms to Explore:**

- o **Coursera and edX:** University-level courses in subjects ranging from business to coding.

- o **Skillshare:** Practical, hands-on classes in art, design, entrepreneurship, and more.

- o **Duolingo:** A gamified app for learning new languages.

- **How to Use:**

  - o Set specific learning goals, such as completing a course within a month.

  - o Dedicate regular time slots for skill development.

  - o Apply what you learn through projects or real-world practice.

Self-Improvement and Mindfulness

Technology can support mental well-being and personal reflection.

- **Apps to Try:**

  - o **Headspace or Calm:** Guided meditation and mindfulness exercises.

  - o **Day One:** A digital journaling app for tracking thoughts, goals, and gratitude.

  - o **Habitica:** Gamifies habit-building to make self-improvement fun and engaging.

- **How to Use:**

  - o Start a daily mindfulness or journaling practice.

  - o Use habit-tracking apps to build consistent, positive routines.

- Explore meditation to reduce stress and improve focus.

3. Leveraging Automation and AI

Streamlining Repetitive Tasks

Automation tools reduce manual effort, freeing up time for more meaningful activities.

- **Tools to Try:**
  - **Zapier:** Connects apps to automate workflows, such as sending email reminders or updating spreadsheets.
  - **IFTTT (If This Then That):** Creates simple automation for daily tasks, like syncing calendars or controlling smart devices.
  - **Grammarly:** Enhances writing by automating grammar and style checks.

AI for Personal Growth

Artificial intelligence can assist with learning and self-improvement.

- **Tools to Explore:**
  - **ChatGPT:** Use AI for brainstorming, learning new topics, or solving complex problems.
  - **Replika:** An AI companion for practicing conversations and emotional reflection.
  - **Anki:** AI-powered flashcards for effective learning and memory retention.
- **How to Use:**

- Automate repetitive tasks to save time and energy.

- Use AI-powered tools for personalized learning or creative problem-solving.

- Incorporate AI assistants to manage reminders, schedules, or note-taking.

4. Building a Balanced Digital Ecosystem

Declutter Your Digital Space

A clutter-free digital environment improves focus and reduces overwhelm.

- **Steps to Declutter:**
  - Organize files and folders with clear naming conventions.

  - Unsubscribe from unnecessary newsletters or email lists.

  - Delete apps or accounts that no longer serve your goals.

Customize Your Experience for Growth

Tailor your digital environment to support your priorities.

- **Suggestions:**
  - Follow inspiring and educational accounts on social media.

  - Use widgets or bookmarks to keep essential tools easily accessible.

  - Turn off notifications for non-essential apps to reduce distractions.

5. Combining Tech with Offline Growth

While technology is a powerful ally, it should complement—not replace—offline growth.

- **Balance Suggestions:**
    - Use tech tools to learn a new skill, then practice it offline (e.g., learning guitar through a tutorial and practicing hands-on).
    - Track fitness goals with apps but prioritize outdoor or gym activities.
    - Use meditation apps to build a habit, then transition to device-free mindfulness practices.

Benefits of Leveraging Technology for Growth

When used effectively, technology can:

- **Increase Efficiency:** Automate tasks and streamline workflows for better time management.
- **Expand Knowledge:** Access a wealth of information and resources for continuous learning.
- **Promote Creativity:** Provide tools for brainstorming, design, and innovation.
- **Enhance Well-Being:** Support mindfulness, goal-setting, and personal reflection.

Conclusion: Harnessing Technology for a Better You

Technology doesn't have to be a source of distraction—it can be a powerful partner in your journey toward productivity and personal growth. By choosing the right tools, setting clear goals, and balancing online and offline efforts, you can unlock new levels of focus, creativity, and self-improvement. Remember, it's not about how much tech you use but how intentionally you use it to enrich your life and achieve your dreams.

Balancing convenience with conscious consumption.

In today's fast-paced, tech-driven world, convenience is at the forefront of almost every decision we make. Technology, apps, and on-demand services have simplified many aspects of life, from food delivery to instant communication. However, the pursuit of convenience often comes at the cost of conscious consumption—mindful choices that consider quality, ethics, and long-term impact. Striking a balance between these two forces can lead to a more intentional, fulfilling, and sustainable way of living.

The Double-Edged Sword of Convenience

Convenience provides undeniable benefits but can also foster mindless habits.

Advantages of Convenience:

- **Time-Saving:** Streamlines tasks like shopping, commuting, and communication.

- **Accessibility:** Makes information, products, and services more readily available.

- **Ease of Use:** Reduces effort and simplifies decision-making.

Challenges of Convenience:

- **Overconsumption:** Encourages impulsive purchases or excessive use of resources.

- **Reduced Quality:** Opting for speed over quality can result in lower satisfaction.

- **Detachment:** Disconnects individuals from the origins of goods and services, such as food production or ethical manufacturing.

Balancing these pros and cons requires intentional effort to prioritize thoughtful consumption over instant gratification.

Principles of Conscious Consumption

Conscious consumption is about making choices that align with your values, needs, and goals. It emphasizes quality, mindfulness, and sustainability over convenience alone.

Key Aspects of Conscious Consumption:

1. **Mindfulness:** Being aware of your habits, needs, and motivations.

2. **Quality Over Quantity:** Choosing products and services that last or provide greater value.

3. **Sustainability:** Supporting practices that minimize environmental and social harm.

4. **Alignment with Values:** Prioritizing purchases and activities that reflect your personal ethics and priorities.

Strategies for Balancing Convenience and Conscious Consumption

1. Pause Before Purchasing

Convenient access to goods and services can lead to impulsive decisions. Develop a habit of pausing before committing to ensure your choices align with your values.

- **Tips:**

- Use a 24-hour rule for non-essential purchases: wait a day before buying to determine if it's truly needed.

- Ask yourself: Does this bring value to my life? Is it a want or a need?

2. Opt for Quality Over Speed

While convenience often prioritizes speed, it's worth considering whether slower, higher-quality options provide more satisfaction and longevity.

- **Examples:**

  - Choose fresh, locally-sourced food over fast food or pre-packaged meals.

  - Invest in durable, ethically-made clothing rather than cheap, disposable fashion.

3. Set Boundaries for Convenience Services

On-demand apps and services are incredibly useful, but over-reliance can lead to unnecessary spending and waste.

- **How to Set Boundaries:**

  - Limit app-based deliveries (e.g., food or groceries) to specific situations, such as busy workdays or special occasions.

  - Combine orders or errands to reduce carbon footprints and save resources.

4. Support Ethical and Sustainable Brands

Convenient doesn't have to mean careless. Seek out companies that prioritize environmental sustainability, fair labor practices, and transparency.

- **Steps to Take:**

  - Research brands before making purchases. Look for certifications like Fair Trade, B Corp, or Carbon Neutral.

  - Support local businesses and artisans, which often prioritize quality and sustainability over mass production.

5. Balance Digital and Physical Consumption

Digital convenience, such as streaming services or online shopping, can be a double-edged sword. Balance virtual experiences with tangible, meaningful ones.

- **Examples:**

  - Visit local bookstores instead of defaulting to online retailers for every purchase.

  - Opt for physical workouts, like yoga classes or hiking, to complement digital fitness apps.

6. Simplify and Declutter

Convenience often leads to excess—too many subscriptions, apps, or gadgets that go unused. Periodic decluttering helps you prioritize what truly matters.

- **How to Simplify:**

  - Cancel unused subscriptions or memberships.

  - Regularly audit your possessions and donate or recycle items you no longer need.

  - Opt for multipurpose tools or services instead of accumulating single-use products.

7. Practice Gratitude and Awareness

Conscious consumption also involves appreciating what you already have. Gratitude fosters contentment and reduces the urge to overindulge in convenience.

- **Suggestions:**
  - Keep a gratitude journal to reflect on the value of your possessions, experiences, and relationships.
  - Focus on experiences over material goods, such as spending time with loved ones or exploring nature.

Technology's Role in Supporting Conscious Consumption

Technology itself can be a tool for balancing convenience and mindfulness when used intentionally.

Apps for Sustainable Choices:

- **Good On You:** Rates fashion brands on ethical and sustainable practices.
- **Too Good To Go:** Connects users with surplus food from restaurants and stores to reduce waste.
- **Think Dirty:** Provides insights into the ingredients and environmental impact of beauty and household products.

Digital Tools for Tracking Habits:

- **Budgeting Apps (e.g., Mint, YNAB):** Help you track spending and align purchases with your values.
- **Carbon Footprint Calculators:** Measure the environmental impact of your consumption habits.

- **Decluttering Tools (e.g., Tody, Sortly):** Help organize and simplify your possessions.

The Benefits of Balancing Convenience and Conscious Consumption

When you find the balance between convenience and intentionality, you can experience a range of benefits:

- **Increased Fulfillment:** Mindful choices bring greater satisfaction and alignment with your values.

- **Better Quality:** Investing in fewer, higher-quality items improves durability and performance.

- **Positive Impact:** Supporting sustainable practices benefits the environment and society.

- **Reduced Waste:** Avoiding overconsumption minimizes clutter and waste.

Conclusion: A Path Toward Intentional Living

Balancing convenience with conscious consumption is about reclaiming control over your choices. It's a mindset that prioritizes thoughtful, meaningful decisions over instant gratification. By integrating these strategies into your life, you can enjoy the benefits of modern convenience while fostering a deeper connection to your values, community, and the planet. Choose wisely, consume mindfully, and live intentionally.

Chapter 10: Building a Sustainable Digital Lifestyle

Creating Long-Term Habits for a Healthy Tech-Life Balance

In today's hyperconnected world, technology is integral to our daily lives. However, overuse or reliance on digital tools can disrupt productivity, mental health, and relationships. Building a sustainable digital lifestyle involves cultivating habits that prioritize intentional tech use while fostering offline connections and personal growth. By creating balance, you can enjoy the benefits of technology without letting it overwhelm your life.

The Importance of a Sustainable Digital Lifestyle

A sustainable digital lifestyle ensures that technology supports, rather than dominates, your well-being and goals. Its key benefits include:

- **Improved Focus:** Reduced digital distractions allow for deeper concentration and productivity.

- **Enhanced Relationships:** Prioritizing offline interactions strengthens personal connections.

- **Better Mental Health:** Mindful tech use reduces stress, anxiety, and feelings of overwhelm.

- **Increased Creativity:** Limiting screen time creates space for hobbies, reflection, and innovation.

Principles of a Healthy Tech-Life Balance

1. **Intentionality:** Use technology with purpose, not as a reflex or distraction.

2. **Boundaries:** Set clear limits on when and where technology is used.

3. **Mindfulness:** Regularly evaluate how digital habits affect your emotions and goals.

4. **Adaptability:** Adjust your habits as your needs and priorities evolve.

Strategies for Creating Long-Term Digital Habits

1. Conduct a Digital Self-Audit

The first step to building sustainable habits is understanding your current relationship with technology.

- **Steps to Audit Your Digital Life:**
    - Track daily screen time using built-in tools like Screen Time (iOS) or Digital Wellbeing (Android).
    - Note how often you check your phone, email, or social media.
    - Reflect on which apps or activities add value and which drain your time and energy.

- **Key Questions:**
    - Are there specific times when I use technology excessively or unproductively?
    - How does my tech use impact my mood, relationships, or productivity?

2. Establish Tech-Free Zones and Times

Designating specific areas and periods as screen-free encourages mindfulness and balance.

- **Examples of Tech-Free Zones:**

- o   The bedroom, to improve sleep quality.

- o   The dining table, to foster meaningful conversations during meals.

- o   Workspaces during focused tasks, to eliminate distractions.

- **Examples of Tech-Free Times:**

  - o   The first hour after waking up to start the day intentionally.

  - o   The last hour before bed to wind down and prepare for restful sleep.

  - o   Regular intervals during family or social gatherings to prioritize in-person connections.

3. Set Digital Boundaries

Boundaries help you create structure around tech use, ensuring it serves your goals.

- **How to Set Boundaries:**

  - o   Schedule specific times to check emails or social media (e.g., twice daily).

  - o   Limit entertainment screen time to a set duration, like one hour per day.

  - o   Use focus modes or app-blocking tools to minimize distractions during work hours.

4. Replace Screen Time with Meaningful Activities

Shift your focus from passive digital consumption to engaging offline activities that bring fulfillment.

- **Suggestions:**

- Explore hobbies like painting, reading, gardening, or cooking.

- Exercise regularly, whether through yoga, hiking, or group sports.

- Spend quality time with loved ones through shared activities or conversations.

5. Practice Digital Minimalism

Embrace a minimalist approach to technology by decluttering your digital environment and prioritizing quality over quantity.

- **Steps to Implement Digital Minimalism:**

  - Uninstall unused apps and reduce the number of notifications.

  - Organize files, emails, and photos to create a streamlined workspace.

  - Follow fewer social media accounts, focusing only on those that inspire or educate.

6. Regularly Reflect and Adjust

Building a sustainable digital lifestyle is an ongoing process. Periodic self-assessment ensures your habits remain aligned with your values and goals.

- **Reflection Questions:**

  - What changes have improved my tech-life balance?

  - Are there new challenges or habits I need to address?

o How can I further refine my relationship with technology?

Leveraging Technology to Support Balance

Technology itself can help you create and maintain a healthier relationship with your devices.

Apps for Productivity and Focus:

- **RescueTime:** Tracks time spent on apps and websites to identify productivity trends.

- **Forest:** Encourages focused work by growing virtual trees during screen-free periods.

- **Cold Turkey:** Blocks distracting websites or apps during scheduled focus times.

Apps for Mindfulness and Well-Being:

- **Headspace or Calm:** Provides guided meditations and mindfulness exercises.

- **Habitica:** Gamifies habit-building to make forming new routines enjoyable.

- **Daylio:** A mood tracker that helps you reflect on how tech use impacts your emotions.

The Long-Term Benefits of a Sustainable Digital Lifestyle

By adopting healthier digital habits, you'll experience lasting positive changes:

1. **More Time for What Matters:** Reclaim hours lost to mindless scrolling and use them for personal growth, relationships, or hobbies.

2. **Stronger Mental Health:** Reduced screen time alleviates stress, anxiety, and digital burnout.

3. **Deeper Connections:** Prioritizing offline interactions strengthens relationships with loved ones.

4. **Enhanced Focus and Productivity:** Intentional tech use eliminates distractions, allowing you to accomplish more.

Practical Steps to Get Started Today

1. **Audit Your Digital Habits:** Spend a week tracking your tech use to identify areas for improvement.

2. **Set One New Boundary:** For example, implement a no-phone rule at the dining table.

3. **Replace One Hour of Screen Time:** Dedicate this time to a meaningful offline activity.

4. **Reflect Weekly:** Assess your progress and adjust your habits as needed.

Conclusion: A Balanced Path Forward

Creating a sustainable digital lifestyle is not about eliminating technology but using it intentionally and mindfully. By cultivating healthy habits and setting clear boundaries, you can harness the benefits of technology while prioritizing your well-being, relationships, and personal growth. Remember, the goal is balance—a tech-life harmony that supports your goals and enriches your life for the long term.

Periodic detox strategies to stay on track.

In a world where technology dominates our daily routines, periodic digital detoxes are essential to maintaining a healthy balance between online and offline life. Unlike one-time detoxes, periodic detox strategies create sustainable habits that help you reset, recharge, and stay aligned with your personal goals. These intentional breaks from screens and digital distractions ensure that technology continues to serve you, rather than control you.

Why Periodic Detoxes Matter

Periodic detoxes allow you to:

- **Reevaluate Your Habits:** Regular breaks offer an opportunity to assess how technology impacts your productivity, relationships, and well-being.

- **Prevent Burnout:** Stepping away from screens reduces mental fatigue and stress caused by overuse.

- **Reconnect with Your Priorities:** Detoxes free up time for meaningful activities, fostering deeper connections and personal growth.

By making detoxing a recurring practice, you can cultivate a healthier, more intentional relationship with technology.

Key Periodic Detox Strategies

1. Set Regular Detox Days

Designate specific days each week or month to unplug from unnecessary digital activity.

- **How to Plan Detox Days:**
  - Choose a day with fewer work or social commitments, such as a Sunday or holiday.
  - Inform family, friends, or colleagues of your plan to ensure understanding and support.
  - Use this time to focus on offline hobbies, spend time outdoors, or connect with loved ones.

- **Example Practice:**
  - Implement "Screen-Free Sundays," where you avoid all non-essential tech use and focus on mindfulness, creativity, or relaxation.

2. Create Mini-Detox Breaks Daily

Incorporate short, intentional tech breaks into your daily routine to reduce screen fatigue.

- **How to Implement Mini-Detox Breaks:**
  - Schedule 10-15 minute breaks for every hour of screen use.
  - Use these breaks to stretch, take a walk, meditate, or simply rest your eyes.
  - Avoid replacing one screen with another (e.g., switching from your computer to your phone).

- **Benefits:**
  - Reduces eye strain and mental fatigue.
  - Encourages mindfulness and physical movement.

3. Plan Digital Sabbaticals

Take an extended break from technology, such as a weekend or a week-long digital detox, to deeply reset your habits.

- **How to Prepare for a Sabbatical:**
  - Plan offline activities, like a vacation, hiking trip, or home improvement project.
  - Log out of social media, turn off non-essential notifications, and delegate urgent work tasks.

o   Keep a journal to reflect on how the detox impacts your focus, mood, and creativity.

- **Frequency Recommendation:**

    o   Consider a quarterly or semi-annual sabbatical to recalibrate your digital habits and realign with your goals.

4. Establish Tech-Free Routines

Incorporate tech-free rituals into your morning or evening routines to create consistency in your detox efforts.

- **Morning Ritual Ideas:**

    o   Start the day with mindfulness practices, such as meditation or journaling, instead of checking your phone.

    o   Spend time outdoors, exercising, or savoring a screen-free breakfast.

- **Evening Ritual Ideas:**

    o   Implement a no-screens policy an hour before bedtime to improve sleep quality.

    o   Use this time to read a physical book, reflect on your day, or enjoy a conversation with a loved one.

5. Detox by Category

Focus on specific types of technology to detox from, targeting the areas where you feel most overwhelmed.

- **Social Media Detox:**

- Take a week off from all social platforms, or limit use to 15 minutes per day.

- Replace scrolling with offline activities, like exercising, reading, or catching up with friends face-to-face.

- **Email Detox:**

  - Check your inbox only twice a day (e.g., morning and afternoon) and avoid email outside these times.

  - Set up autoresponders to manage expectations during your detox.

- **Streaming Detox:**

  - Replace binge-watching with offline entertainment, such as board games or creative hobbies.

  - Limit TV or streaming to one show or movie per day.

6. Use Tech to Support Your Detox

Leverage apps and tools that encourage mindfulness and limit digital distractions.

- **Recommended Apps:**

  - **Forest:** Helps you focus by growing virtual trees during screen-free time.

  - **Freedom:** Blocks distracting websites or apps during your detox.

  - **Headspace or Calm:** Offers guided meditations to help you relax and recharge.

- **How to Use:**
  - Schedule focus sessions using these tools during work hours.
  - Set app or screen time limits to reinforce your detox boundaries.

7. Reflect on Each Detox

After each detox, take time to evaluate its impact and identify areas for improvement.

- **Reflection Questions:**
  - What challenges did I face during the detox, and how did I overcome them?
  - How did the detox improve my focus, mood, or relationships?
  - What new habits or boundaries can I implement going forward?

- **Actionable Steps:**
  - Write down your reflections in a journal.
  - Use insights from your detox to adjust your daily digital habits.

Benefits of Periodic Digital Detoxes

By integrating periodic detox strategies into your routine, you can experience:

1. **Increased Clarity:** Reduced digital noise enhances focus and decision-making.

2. **Stronger Connections:** Prioritizing offline interactions deepens relationships with loved ones.

3. **Greater Productivity:** Eliminating distractions frees up time for meaningful activities.

4. **Improved Well-Being:** Regular breaks from screens reduce stress and promote mindfulness.

5. **Enhanced Creativity:** Stepping away from technology fosters fresh ideas and innovation.

Getting Started with Periodic Detoxing

1. **Schedule Your First Detox:** Choose a day or weekend to go screen-free and plan offline activities.

2. **Start Small:** Begin with daily mini-detox breaks or tech-free routines to build consistency.

3. **Track Progress:** Reflect on each detox experience to identify what works and refine your approach.

Conclusion: A Lifelong Practice for Digital Balance

Periodic detoxes are not about rejecting technology but about using it more intentionally. By incorporating these strategies into your life, you can maintain a healthy balance between digital and offline worlds, ensuring that technology enhances, rather than detracts from, your overall well-being. Make periodic detoxing a regular part of your routine, and enjoy the freedom, clarity, and fulfillment it brings.

Celebrating the freedom and clarity of a less digital life.

In a world where screens dominate our attention and technology infiltrates every corner of our lives, choosing to step back from the digital noise is an act of empowerment. A less digital life is not about abandoning technology but about reclaiming control, presence, and purpose. It's about celebrating the freedom and clarity that comes from living intentionally and creating space for what truly matters.

The Freedom of a Less Digital Life

1. Reclaiming Your Time

Reducing screen time gives you the freedom to direct your energy toward meaningful activities.

- **Benefits:**
  - More time for hobbies, passions, and creative pursuits.
  - The ability to fully engage in face-to-face conversations and relationships.
  - The joy of experiencing life without the constant interruption of notifications.

2. Breaking Free from Overstimulation

Digital devices bombard us with information, often leading to stress and overwhelm. A less digital life offers the peace that comes with a quieter, less cluttered mind.

- **Benefits:**
  - Less mental fatigue from endless scrolling and multitasking.
  - A calmer, more focused approach to daily tasks.
  - Greater emotional balance, unclouded by digital comparison or negativity.

3. Rediscovering Autonomy

By setting boundaries with technology, you reclaim control over how you spend your time and attention.

- **Benefits:**
  - Freedom from the algorithm-driven loops that dictate your online behavior.
  - A renewed sense of agency in choosing activities that align with your values.
  - The ability to live life on your terms, rather than according to digital demands.

The Clarity of a Less Digital Life

1. Enhanced Presence

Stepping away from screens allows you to be fully present in the moment, whether it's enjoying a sunset, savoring a meal, or listening to a loved one.

- **How It Feels:**
  - Conversations become deeper and more meaningful.
  - Experiences are richer when you're not distracted by capturing them for social media.
  - Life slows down, and you notice the beauty in everyday moments.

2. Sharper Focus

A less digital life eliminates distractions, making room for clarity and intentionality.

- **How It Feels:**
  - You can immerse yourself in tasks without the constant pull of notifications.

- Long-term goals and priorities become clearer when you're not consumed by digital noise.

- Problem-solving and creativity flourish in a distraction-free environment.

3. Authentic Self-Reflection

Without the influence of online personas or curated feeds, you can reconnect with your true self.

- **How It Feels:**

    - Greater self-awareness as you tune in to your own thoughts and emotions.

    - Confidence grows when your self-worth isn't tied to likes or comments.

    - Time for introspection helps you align your actions with your core values.

Ways to Celebrate a Less Digital Life

1. Embrace Offline Activities

Fill the space created by reduced screen time with activities that bring joy and fulfillment.

- **Ideas:**

    - Take up a hobby like painting, cooking, or gardening.

    - Spend more time outdoors, enjoying the restorative power of nature.

    - Organize game nights, book clubs, or potlucks with friends and family.

2. Reflect on Your Journey

Take time to acknowledge the positive changes a less digital life has brought.

- **Reflection Prompts:**
    - What have I gained by spending less time online?
    - How has my focus, mood, or relationships improved?
    - What offline experiences have brought me the most joy?

3. Share Your Success

Celebrate your journey by sharing your experiences with others, inspiring them to consider their own relationship with technology.

- **Ways to Share:**
    - Host a digital detox challenge with friends or family.
    - Write about your journey in a blog, journal, or social media post.
    - Discuss your favorite offline activities with loved ones.

4. Reward Yourself

Mark milestones in your digital detox journey with meaningful rewards.

- **Examples:**
    - Treat yourself to a weekend getaway or a special outing.

- o Invest in tools or resources that support your offline interests, like art supplies or hiking gear.

- o Celebrate with a "tech-free" day filled with activities you love.

The Long-Term Impact of a Less Digital Life

1. Greater Fulfillment

A life less tethered to screens opens the door to deeper satisfaction and happiness.

- **Why It Matters:**

  - o You spend time on activities and relationships that truly matter.

  - o The reduced pace of life allows for savoring and appreciating moments.

2. Stronger Connections

Focusing on in-person interactions strengthens bonds with loved ones.

- **Why It Matters:**

  - o Eye contact, touch, and shared experiences foster intimacy and trust.

  - o Being present shows others that you value their time and attention.

3. Sustainable Balance

As you integrate a less digital lifestyle into your routine, it becomes a sustainable way of living.

- **Why It Matters:**

- Long-term habits ensure that technology supports rather than distracts from your goals.

- Balance between online and offline worlds brings stability and peace of mind.

Conclusion: Rediscovering Life Beyond Screens

Celebrating the freedom and clarity of a less digital life is about embracing what technology cannot replicate—genuine connections, personal growth, and the beauty of the present moment. By choosing to step away from screens, you open the door to a life filled with purpose, joy, and authenticity. The rewards are not just fleeting moments of peace but a profound, lasting sense of fulfillment. Take a moment to savor the richness of living intentionally and remember that the best parts of life often happen when you look up from your screen.

Chapter 11: Inspiring Stories of Transformation

Personal Accounts of Successful Detox Journeys

Embarking on a digital detox can feel daunting, but the stories of those who have taken the leap and reaped the rewards offer inspiration and motivation. These real-life accounts showcase the power of intentional living, highlighting the profound impact that reducing screen time can have on focus, relationships, mental health, and personal fulfillment.

1. Lisa: Reclaiming Creativity Through a Digital Detox

Lisa, a graphic designer, found herself trapped in a cycle of constant scrolling and comparison on social media. Her evenings were spent consuming other creators' work, leaving her too drained to work on her passion projects.

Her Journey:

- Lisa started with a 7-day social media detox, uninstalling all social apps from her phone.

- She replaced scrolling with journaling and sketching, rediscovering her love for drawing.

- By the end of the week, Lisa felt less overwhelmed and more inspired to pursue her own creative ideas.

The Outcome:

Lisa now dedicates her evenings to working on personal art projects. She uses social media intentionally, limiting her usage to 30 minutes daily for professional networking and inspiration.

- **Her Reflection:**
  "Detoxing from social media wasn't easy at first, but it was transformative. It reminded me that I don't need to consume endlessly to create meaningfully."

2. James: Strengthening Family Bonds

James, a busy entrepreneur, realized that his constant attachment to his phone was straining his relationship with his wife and two young children. Despite being physically present at home, he was often mentally checked out, responding to emails or scrolling news feeds.

His Journey:

- James implemented tech-free zones in his home, starting with the dining room and living room.

- He established a nightly ritual of reading bedtime stories to his kids and engaging in screen-free conversations with his wife.

- He also began a "no-phone Sundays" policy, dedicating the entire day to family activities.

The Outcome:

James noticed a dramatic improvement in his relationships. His children were more open with him, and his wife appreciated the quality time they now shared.

- **His Reflection:**
  "I used to think my phone kept me connected, but it was actually disconnecting me from the people who matter most. The detox gave me back my family."

3. Priya: Overcoming Burnout with Intentional Tech Use

As a marketing executive, Priya was constantly on her laptop and phone, juggling work emails, social media campaigns, and personal chats. She began to experience burnout, with constant headaches and difficulty sleeping.

Her Journey:

- Priya committed to a one-month digital detox, focusing on work-life balance.

- She set strict work hours, avoiding emails and messages after 6 PM.

- Priya also replaced her evening screen time with meditation and yoga.

The Outcome:

Within weeks, Priya felt more energized and in control of her schedule. Her sleep improved, and she started enjoying her downtime without the guilt of leaving tasks unfinished.

- **Her Reflection:**
  "The detox helped me see that being always 'on' wasn't sustainable. Now, I'm more productive during work hours and more present in my personal life."

4. Ahmed: Rebuilding Mental Clarity

Ahmed, a college student, struggled with focus and procrastination due to excessive screen time. He spent hours gaming and scrolling through memes, often delaying his assignments until the last minute.

His Journey:

- Ahmed began with a 30-day gaming detox, replacing his gaming sessions with reading and studying in the library.

- He used apps like Forest to stay focused during study sessions, rewarding himself with screen-free breaks outdoors.

- Ahmed also joined a local book club to build offline connections.

The Outcome:

Ahmed's grades improved significantly, and he developed a newfound love for literature. The detox not only helped him academically but also boosted his confidence and sense of purpose.

- **His Reflection:**
  "I didn't realize how much gaming was holding me back until I took a break. The detox gave me clarity and reminded me of my potential."

5. Sofia: Finding Peace and Purpose

Sofia, a retired teacher, felt that her days were slipping away in a haze of TV shows, online shopping, and endless news consumption. She longed for more meaningful ways to spend her time but didn't know where to start.

Her Journey:

- Sofia initiated a week-long digital detox, turning off her TV and setting her phone to airplane mode.

- She rediscovered old hobbies like knitting and gardening, which brought her immense joy.

- Sofia also started volunteering at a local shelter, dedicating her mornings to helping others.

The Outcome:

Sofia's days became more purposeful and fulfilling. She continued to limit her screen time, prioritizing activities that enriched her life and her community.

- **Her Reflection:**
  "The detox was like waking up from a fog. I'm now living intentionally and focusing on what truly matters."

Key Takeaways from These Transformations

1. **Start Small:** Each person began their journey with manageable steps, like setting boundaries or detoxing for a week.

2. **Replace, Don't Remove:** They filled the gap left by screens with meaningful offline activities.

3. **Focus on What Matters:** Detoxing allowed them to reconnect with creativity, relationships, and personal growth.

4. **Make It Sustainable:** The transformations were not just about temporary fixes but long-term lifestyle changes.

Conclusion: The Power of Personal Transformation

These inspiring stories demonstrate that a digital detox isn't just about breaking free from screens—it's about reclaiming your time, energy, and purpose. Whether it's nurturing relationships, rediscovering passions, or finding mental clarity, the rewards of intentional living are profound. Let these journeys inspire your own path toward balance, freedom, and a less digital life filled with meaning and connection.

Lessons learned and wisdom shared from real people.

The journey to balancing technology and life is deeply personal, yet the lessons learned along the way often resonate universally. Real stories from individuals who have successfully navigated digital detoxes and intentional tech use offer profound wisdom and practical insights. These lessons highlight the transformative power of mindfulness, boundaries, and prioritizing what truly matters.

Lesson 1: Awareness is the First Step

Wisdom Shared by Sarah, a Busy Professional
Sarah, a marketing executive, realized she was spending over six hours daily on her phone, much of it on social media. She initially felt overwhelmed by the idea of cutting back but began with one simple step: tracking her usage.

- **Her Lesson:**
  "I didn't realize how much time I was wasting until I saw the numbers. Awareness is powerful—it gave me the clarity to make changes without feeling guilty."

- **Takeaway:**
  Start by observing your habits. Use tracking tools or keep a digital journal to understand how, when, and why you use technology. Awareness lays the foundation for meaningful change.

Lesson 2: Replace Scrolling with Meaningful Activities

Wisdom Shared by David, an Aspiring Writer
David often felt drained and uninspired after hours of aimless scrolling. During his digital detox, he decided to channel that time into writing—a passion he'd neglected for years.

- **His Lesson:**
  "The urge to scroll is just a habit. When I replaced it with writing, I not only felt more fulfilled but also rediscovered something I truly love."

- **Takeaway:**
  Don't just remove screen time—replace it with activities that enrich your life, like hobbies, exercise, or spending time with loved ones.

Lesson 3: Boundaries Create Freedom

Wisdom Shared by Mia, a Mother of Two

Mia struggled with the constant pull of notifications, which often distracted her from time with her children. She implemented a no-phone policy during family dinners and bedtime routines.

- **Her Lesson:**
  "I thought boundaries would feel restrictive, but they actually gave me more freedom to be present with my family. The moments I used to miss are now the highlights of my day."

- **Takeaway:**
  Boundaries, such as designated tech-free zones or times, protect what matters most and help you regain control of your attention.

Lesson 4: Small Changes Add Up

Wisdom Shared by Alex, a College Student

Alex felt overwhelmed by the idea of a full digital detox, so he started with mini-detoxes—15 minutes of phone-free time in the morning and before bed.

- **His Lesson:**
  "I didn't need a drastic overhaul to see results. Small, consistent changes made it easier to stick with the process and stay motivated."

- **Takeaway:**
  Incremental steps, like starting with short breaks or reducing app usage, can lead to significant improvements over time.

Lesson 5: Social Media is a Tool, Not a Necessity

Wisdom Shared by Priya, a Small Business Owner

Priya initially resisted detoxing from social media, believing it was essential for her business. However, after limiting her usage to specific times and automating posts, she discovered a healthier balance.

- **Her Lesson:**
  "Social media is a tool, not my life. Once I started using it intentionally, I stopped feeling like it was using me."

- **Takeaway:**
  View social media as a means to an end, whether for work or connection, rather than a constant obligation. Use it purposefully and limit unnecessary engagement.

Lesson 6: Presence is Priceless

Wisdom Shared by Liam, a Retiree

Liam realized he spent more time on his tablet than engaging with his grandchildren during their visits. After committing to a digital detox, he found himself fully immersed in their play and conversations.

- **His Lesson:**
  "Being present isn't about doing more; it's about simply showing up without distractions. My relationships feel richer because of it."

- **Takeaway:**
  Put devices aside during face-to-face interactions to create deeper, more meaningful connections.

Lesson 7: Technology Can Support Balance

Wisdom Shared by Elena, a Teacher

Elena didn't want to abandon technology entirely but sought ways to make it work for her. She used focus apps and scheduling tools to create a structured, distraction-free work environment.

- **Her Lesson:**
  "Technology isn't the enemy—it's how you use it. When I set limits and used apps to support my goals, my productivity soared."

- **Takeaway:**
  Use technology intentionally. Leverage tools like focus apps, time trackers, and notification settings to stay on track without overindulging.

Lesson 8: Reflection Reinforces Growth

Wisdom Shared by Sofia, a Volunteer

Sofia kept a journal throughout her detox, recording her thoughts and progress. Reflecting on her experiences helped her identify what worked and where she could improve.

- **Her Lesson:**
  "Reflection turned my detox into a journey of self-discovery. I learned so much about what truly matters to me."

- **Takeaway:**
  Regularly reflect on your detox journey. Write down what you've gained, the challenges you've faced, and the changes you'd like to sustain.

Lesson 9: The World Feels Bigger Offline

Wisdom Shared by Ahmed, an Outdoor Enthusiast

After a week-long detox, Ahmed spent more time outdoors, hiking and exploring new places. He realized how much he'd been missing while glued to screens.

- **His Lesson:**
  "When I unplugged, I rediscovered the beauty of the real world. The screen shrinks your life, but stepping away expands it."

- **Takeaway:**
  Engage with the physical world around you—nature, people, and experiences. These moments are irreplaceable.

Lesson 10: A Less Digital Life is a More Intentional Life

Wisdom Shared by Clara, a Wellness Coach
Clara found that reducing her digital dependency helped her focus on aligning her actions with her values.

- **Her Lesson:**
  "Living with less technology didn't mean doing less—it meant doing what truly matters with more intention and joy."

- **Takeaway:**
  A less digital life isn't about deprivation—it's about prioritizing meaningful, intentional living over mindless consumption.

Conclusion: Collective Wisdom for Personal Growth

The lessons shared by real people highlight the transformative power of intentional tech use and digital detoxing. Whether it's through setting boundaries, reflecting on habits, or replacing screen time with meaningful activities, these stories remind us that balance is possible. The journey to a healthier relationship with technology starts with small steps, guided by the wisdom and experiences of those who've walked the path before us. Their stories can inspire and empower you to create your own transformation.

Motivation to stay committed to your detox path.

Embarking on a digital detox journey is an empowering step toward reclaiming balance, focus, and connection in your life. However, staying committed can be challenging, especially in a world designed to keep you plugged in. Maintaining motivation requires a clear vision of your goals, consistent reminders of your progress, and strategies to overcome obstacles. Here's how to stay inspired and steadfast on your detox path.

1. Remind Yourself of Your "Why"

Every journey starts with a purpose. Reconnect with the reasons you began your detox journey to fuel your motivation.

- **Reflection Questions:**
    - What was the tipping point that led me to pursue a digital detox?
    - How do I want my life to improve by reducing screen time?
    - What benefits have I already noticed since starting my detox?

- **Actionable Tip:**
  Write down your "why" and place it somewhere visible—on your desk, mirror, or as a phone wallpaper—to serve as a daily reminder.

2. Visualize the Positive Outcomes

Focus on the benefits you'll achieve by sticking to your detox path. Visualization strengthens your resolve and keeps your end goals in sight.

- **Examples of Positive Outcomes:**

- o More meaningful connections with family and friends.

- o Improved mental clarity, focus, and creativity.

- o Greater time and energy for hobbies, passions, and personal growth.

- **Actionable Tip:**
  Create a vision board with images or phrases that represent your goals and the life you're working toward.

3. Track Your Progress

Monitoring your achievements reinforces your motivation by showing how far you've come.

- **How to Track Progress:**

  - o Use a habit tracker app to log screen-free days or time spent on offline activities.

  - o Keep a journal to document the emotional and practical benefits of your detox.

  - o Celebrate milestones, like completing your first week of reduced screen time or reaching a personal goal.

- **Actionable Tip:**
  Review your progress weekly and reflect on the improvements in your focus, mood, and relationships.

4. Set Small, Achievable Goals

Breaking your detox journey into smaller steps makes it less daunting and provides frequent opportunities for success.

- **Examples of Goals:**

- o Reduce social media use by 30 minutes per day.

- o Implement a tech-free hour each evening.

- o Spend one day per week without non-essential screen time.

- **Actionable Tip:**
  Celebrate small wins with meaningful rewards, like treating yourself to a favorite activity or enjoying a screen-free outing.

5. Surround Yourself with Support

Building a community of like-minded individuals can keep you motivated and accountable.

- **How to Find Support:**

  - o Share your detox goals with friends or family and ask for their encouragement.

  - o Join online or in-person groups focused on digital mindfulness or intentional living.

  - o Partner with an accountability buddy to check in on each other's progress.

- **Actionable Tip:**
  Discuss your challenges and successes with your support network regularly. Their encouragement can help you stay on track.

6. Focus on the Present Moment

Detoxing isn't just about reducing screen time—it's about embracing the joys of being present.

- **How to Stay Present:**

- o Practice mindfulness through meditation or breathing exercises.

- o Engage fully in offline activities, like cooking, gardening, or spending time outdoors.

- o Notice the sensory details of your surroundings— the sounds, sights, and textures that digital distractions often drown out.

- **Actionable Tip:**
  Start each day with a mindful intention to fully experience one offline moment, like a morning walk or sharing a meal with loved ones.

7. Reframe Challenges as Opportunities

It's natural to face moments of temptation or frustration during a detox. Reframe these challenges as opportunities to strengthen your commitment.

- **Examples of Reframes:**

  - o Feeling the urge to scroll? View it as a chance to practice self-discipline.

  - o Struggling with boredom? Use it as an opportunity to explore a new hobby or revisit an old passion.

- **Actionable Tip:**
  When challenges arise, pause and remind yourself of how overcoming them contributes to your growth.

8. Focus on What You're Gaining, Not Losing

Instead of dwelling on what you're giving up, celebrate the benefits you're gaining through your detox journey.

- **Shift Your Perspective:**
    - Replace "I can't check my phone" with "I have time to connect with loved ones."
    - Replace "I'm missing out online" with "I'm fully present in the real world."
- **Actionable Tip:**
  Keep a gratitude journal to highlight the positive changes your detox has brought into your life.

9. Revisit Inspirational Stories

Learning about others who have successfully transformed their relationship with technology can reignite your motivation.

- **Where to Find Inspiration:**
    - Read books or blogs about digital mindfulness and detox journeys.
    - Watch documentaries or listen to podcasts that explore the benefits of unplugging.
    - Reflect on your own progress and how far you've come.
- **Actionable Tip:**
  Create a list of motivational quotes or stories to revisit when you need encouragement.

10. Remind Yourself It's a Journey, Not a Race

Building a healthier relationship with technology is a lifelong process. Allow yourself grace and flexibility as you navigate the ups and downs.

- **Mindset to Adopt:**

- o Progress is more important than perfection.

- o Slip-ups are opportunities to learn, not reasons to quit.

- **Actionable Tip:**
  Reflect on setbacks with curiosity rather than judgment, and adjust your approach as needed.

Conclusion: The Rewards of Staying Committed

Staying committed to your detox path requires intention, persistence, and a focus on the bigger picture. By celebrating small victories, leaning on support, and embracing the joys of a less digital life, you can maintain the motivation to achieve your goals. Remember, every step forward—no matter how small—brings you closer to the freedom, clarity, and fulfillment that come from living intentionally in a tech-saturated world. Stay the course, and the rewards will be worth it.

Conclusion: The New You

How Digital Detoxing Unlocks Your True Potential

Completing your digital detox journey is more than just a lifestyle change—it's a transformative process that reveals the best version of yourself. By stepping away from the constant buzz of notifications and the allure of screens, you've created space to reconnect with your goals, passions, and relationships. This is the "new you"—a more intentional, focused, and fulfilled individual, ready to harness the full potential of life both on and offline.

Rediscovering What Matters

One of the most profound outcomes of digital detoxing is the clarity it brings to what truly matters. Without the distractions of endless scrolling and digital noise, you've reconnected with:

- **Your Purpose:** You've gained the mental clarity to prioritize what aligns with your values and aspirations.

- **Your Relationships:** You've deepened bonds with family and friends through genuine, screen-free interactions.

- **Your Passions:** You've rediscovered hobbies, creativity, and activities that bring joy and fulfillment.

The Benefits of Intentional Living

Through detoxing, you've unlocked a life that is richer, simpler, and more purposeful. These benefits extend far beyond the absence of screens:

1. Freedom from Distraction

You've taken back control of your time and attention, breaking free from the constant pull of notifications and algorithms.

- **What This Means:** You can focus deeply on tasks, be present in the moment, and enjoy uninterrupted periods of creativity and productivity.

2. Emotional Balance

Stepping away from digital stressors like comparison, FOMO, and information overload has improved your emotional well-being.

- **What This Means:** You feel calmer, more confident, and less reactive to external pressures.

3. Greater Fulfillment

Without screens filling every idle moment, you've filled your life with meaningful activities and experiences.

- **What This Means:** You're living intentionally, savoring each day, and investing in what truly enriches your life.

Unlocking Your True Potential

By embracing a more intentional relationship with technology, you've created the foundation for unlocking your full potential.

1. Enhanced Productivity

With fewer distractions, you've developed the ability to focus deeply on your goals and achieve more in less time.

- **Your Growth:** You've learned to prioritize tasks, manage time effectively, and work with purpose.

2. Improved Relationships

Your presence in offline interactions has strengthened your connections with loved ones and colleagues.

- **Your Growth:** You've become a better communicator, listener, and partner in both personal and professional relationships.

3. Reignited Creativity

Detoxing has cleared mental clutter, allowing your imagination and innovation to flourish.

- **Your Growth:** You've rekindled passions, explored new hobbies, and created opportunities for personal and professional breakthroughs.

Sustaining Your New Life

The journey doesn't end here—maintaining your progress requires commitment and mindfulness. Here's how to sustain the new you:

1. Regular Digital Detoxes

Make periodic detoxes a part of your routine to recalibrate and stay balanced.

- **Actionable Tip:** Schedule tech-free weekends, daily breaks, or quarterly detoxes to stay grounded.

2. Set Boundaries with Technology

Continue to use screens intentionally, ensuring they enhance rather than dominate your life.

- **Actionable Tip:** Create tech-free zones, set time limits, and curate your digital environment.

3. Celebrate Your Wins

Acknowledge the progress you've made and the positive changes you've experienced.

- **Actionable Tip:** Reflect on your journey through journaling or share your story with others to inspire them.

Embracing the New You

The "new you" is more than a person who uses technology less—it's someone who lives more intentionally, more fully, and more authentically. By taking charge of your digital habits, you've paved the way for a life of clarity, connection, and creativity.

- **You've learned to:**
  - Focus on what matters most.
  - Cultivate meaningful relationships.
  - Unlock your potential for growth and achievement.

This is the power of a digital detox—it doesn't just reduce your screen time; it reveals your true self.

Moving Forward

As you step into this new chapter, remember that the tools and insights you've gained are yours to keep. Technology will always be a part of modern life, but now you have the wisdom to use it intentionally, the strength to set boundaries, and the clarity to prioritize what truly matters.

You've transformed your relationship with technology—and in doing so, you've transformed your life. The new you is here, ready to embrace a life of purpose, balance, and unlimited potential.

Embracing a life of balance, presence, and purpose.

In a fast-paced, hyperconnected world, the pursuit of balance, presence, and purpose is more important than ever. Technology offers incredible convenience, but its constant presence can cloud our ability to live intentionally. By redefining how we interact with the digital world, we can create a life that prioritizes meaningful connections, mindful living, and the pursuit of what truly matters.

Finding Balance: Aligning Priorities with Action

Balance isn't about perfection; it's about making intentional choices that reflect your values and priorities. It requires creating boundaries, managing your time effectively, and ensuring that every aspect of your life receives the attention it deserves.

How to Cultivate Balance:

1. **Set Clear Boundaries:** Define when and where technology is allowed in your life (e.g., tech-free meals or evenings).

2. **Prioritize What Matters:** Align your daily actions with your long-term goals, whether it's fostering relationships, advancing your career, or nurturing your health.

3. **Schedule Downtime:** Balance isn't just about productivity—it's also about rest. Dedicate time for self-care, hobbies, and relaxation.

The Benefits of Balance:

- Reduced stress and overwhelm.

- More time and energy for meaningful activities.

- A sense of control over your life and decisions.

Living with Presence: Fully Engaging in the Moment

Presence is about being fully engaged in what you're doing, whether it's listening to a loved one, working on a project, or savoring a quiet moment. It's the antidote to distraction, helping you connect deeply with yourself and others.

How to Cultivate Presence:

1. **Practice Mindfulness:** Start your day with mindful breathing or meditation to ground yourself.

2. **Engage Fully:** Put away devices during conversations or activities to give your undivided attention.

3. **Notice the Details:** Pay attention to the sights, sounds, and sensations of your surroundings—be curious and observant.

The Benefits of Presence:

- Deeper, more meaningful relationships.

- Improved focus and productivity.

- A greater appreciation for life's small joys.

Living with Purpose: Aligning Actions with Values

Purpose is the guiding force that gives meaning to your actions. It's about knowing what you stand for, setting meaningful goals, and dedicating your time to pursuits that align with your values.

How to Cultivate Purpose:

1. **Clarify Your Values:** Reflect on what matters most to you—family, creativity, health, community, or personal growth.

2. **Set Intentional Goals:** Break down long-term aspirations into achievable steps that align with your purpose.

3. **Reflect Regularly:** Take time to assess whether your daily actions support your larger purpose and adjust as needed.

The Benefits of Purpose:

- A clear sense of direction and motivation.

- Greater resilience in the face of challenges.

- A life filled with meaning and satisfaction.

Integrating Balance, Presence, and Purpose

The true power of these principles lies in how they complement and reinforce each other:

- **Balance Provides the Foundation:** When you balance your time and energy, you create the space to live with presence and pursue your purpose.

- **Presence Deepens Your Experience:** Being present allows you to fully engage in meaningful activities and relationships, enriching your pursuit of purpose.

- **Purpose Guides Your Choices:** A clear sense of purpose ensures that your time and energy are directed toward what truly matters, making balance and presence more attainable.

Practical Steps to Embrace This Life

1. Create Daily Rituals

Incorporate practices that support balance, presence, and purpose into your daily routine.

- **Examples:**
  - Start the morning with gratitude journaling or goal-setting.
  - Dedicate specific blocks of time to focused work, family, and self-care.
  - Reflect in the evening on what went well and what aligns with your purpose.

2. Limit Digital Overload

Reduce the influence of technology by setting boundaries and curating your digital environment.

- **Examples:**
  - Turn off non-essential notifications to minimize distractions.
  - Limit screen time during key moments of the day, such as meals or relaxation periods.
  - Use apps intentionally, focusing only on those that add value to your life.

3. Celebrate Small Wins

Recognize and appreciate the progress you make toward balance, presence, and purpose, no matter how small.

- **Examples:**
  - Acknowledge moments of focus or mindfulness.
  - Celebrate days when you feel aligned with your purpose.
  - Share your successes with loved ones for added encouragement.

The Transformational Power of This Path

Choosing to live a life of balance, presence, and purpose unlocks your potential and leads to a richer, more fulfilling existence. You'll experience:

- **More Meaningful Connections:** Presence strengthens bonds with loved ones, friends, and colleagues.

- **Greater Resilience:** Balance and purpose provide stability and motivation during challenging times.

- **Increased Fulfillment:** Living intentionally ensures that your time and energy are spent on what truly matters.

Conclusion: The Joy of Intentional Living

Embracing balance, presence, and purpose is not a destination but a continuous journey of self-discovery and growth. It's about reclaiming your life from distractions, aligning your actions with your values, and fully engaging with the world around you.

Every step you take toward this way of living brings you closer to a life filled with meaning, connection, and joy. By prioritizing what matters most and living with intention, you'll create a life that reflects your true self—a life where you're not just surviving but truly thriving.

A final call to action: Empowering yourself to thrive in the digital age.

The digital age offers incredible opportunities for connection, creativity, and growth. Yet, it also presents challenges—distractions, overconsumption, and the risk of losing sight of what truly matters. This is your moment to take charge, to shape your digital habits intentionally, and to build a life that embraces the best of technology without being consumed by it. The power to thrive in the digital age lies in your hands.

Step 1: Reclaim Control

Empowering yourself starts with reclaiming control over your time, attention, and choices. The digital world is designed to demand your focus, but you have the agency to decide how, when, and why you engage with it.

Action Points:

- **Set Boundaries:** Create specific times for tech use and stick to them.

- **Be Intentional:** Use technology as a tool to support your goals, not as a default escape or distraction.

- **Limit Notifications:** Reduce interruptions by turning off non-essential alerts.

Step 2: Prioritize What Matters

In the rush of digital interactions, it's easy to lose sight of what truly matters—relationships, health, creativity, and personal growth. Use your detox journey as a foundation to refocus on your values.

Action Points:

- **Define Your Values:** Reflect on what's most important to you and align your actions with those priorities.

- **Make Time for Connections:** Dedicate quality, screen-free time to family, friends, and loved ones.

- **Invest in Growth:** Pursue offline hobbies, learn new skills, and engage in activities that bring you joy.

Step 3: Build Resilience Against Digital Overload

The digital age is fast-paced and relentless, but resilience allows you to navigate it without feeling overwhelmed. Develop habits and strategies that protect your mental health and keep you grounded.

Action Points:

- **Practice Mindfulness:** Incorporate daily practices like meditation or journaling to stay present.

- **Take Breaks:** Regularly step away from screens to recharge your energy and creativity.

- **Cultivate Gratitude:** Focus on the positive aspects of your life that go beyond the digital world.

Step 4: Use Technology for Good

Technology isn't the enemy—it's a tool. When used intentionally, it can amplify your productivity, strengthen relationships, and fuel personal growth.

Action Points:

- **Leverage Productivity Tools:** Use apps to organize tasks, manage time, and track progress toward your goals.

- **Curate Your Digital Environment:** Follow accounts and platforms that inspire, educate, and align with your values.

- **Support Your Community:** Use technology to advocate for causes, share knowledge, and connect with others meaningfully.

Step 5: Stay Committed to Your Journey

Empowerment is a continuous process. Staying intentional and reflective ensures that your digital habits remain aligned with your vision for a balanced, purposeful life.

Action Points:

- **Reflect Regularly:** Periodically review your digital habits and adjust them as needed.

- **Celebrate Progress:** Acknowledge the small victories that show how far you've come.

- **Inspire Others:** Share your journey to encourage others to take charge of their digital lives.

The Transformation Awaits

Empowering yourself to thrive in the digital age is not about rejecting technology—it's about embracing it mindfully and intentionally. By reclaiming control, prioritizing what matters, and using technology for good, you can lead a life that's rich in connection, creativity, and fulfillment.

- **Imagine:** A life where you wake up with clarity, spend your days aligned with your goals, and end your evenings with peace of mind.

- **Envision:** A future where your digital habits serve you rather than control you.

- **Act:** The journey begins now—one intentional choice at a time.

Your Call to Action

Take the first step today. Reflect on your digital habits, set a small but meaningful goal, and commit to living with purpose. Empower yourself to thrive—not just survive—in the digital age. The tools are in your hands, and the possibilities are endless.

Your life is waiting. Make it extraordinary.

References

Books and Academic Sources

1. **Newport, Cal. (2019).** *Digital Minimalism: Choosing a Focused Life in a Noisy World.* Portfolio/Penguin.

    o   Explores how intentional digital habits can lead to a more focused and meaningful life.

2. **Price, Catherine. (2018).** *How to Break Up with Your Phone: The 30-Day Plan to Take Back Your Life.* Ten Speed Press.

    o   Offers practical steps to regain control over your phone use and create healthier digital habits.

3. **Turkle, Sherry. (2015).** *Reclaiming Conversation: The Power of Talk in a Digital Age.* Penguin Press.

    o   Examines how digital communication affects human relationships and the importance of face-to-face conversation.

4. **Carr, Nicholas. (2010).** *The Shallows: What the Internet Is Doing to Our Brains.* W. W. Norton & Company.

    o   Investigates how digital media reshapes cognitive functions and impacts our ability to focus.

5. **Boyd, Dana. (2014).** *It's Complicated: The Social Lives of Networked Teens.* Yale University Press.

    o   Analyzes how social media shapes the experiences of teenagers and their relationships with technology.

Scientific Studies and Research Papers

6. **Rosen, Larry D., Whaling, Kelly, Carrier, L. Mark, Cheever, Nancy A., & Rokkum, John. (2013).** *The Media and Technology Usage and Attitudes Scale: An Empirical Investigation. Computers in Human Behavior, 29*(6), 2501-2511.

   o Introduces a scale to measure media and technology usage and its psychological effects.

7. **Kushlev, Kostadin, Proulx, Joshua D., & Dunn, Elizabeth W. (2016).** *"Silence Your Phones": Smartphone Notifications Increase Inattention and Hyperactivity Symptoms. Computers in Human Behavior, 63,* 445-451.

   o Explores the impact of smartphone notifications on attention and behavior.

8. **Twenge, Jean M., & Campbell, W. Keith. (2018).** *The Narcissism Epidemic: Living in the Age of Entitlement.* Free Press.

   o Discusses how social media contributes to changes in self-perception and interpersonal dynamics.

9. **Alter, Adam. (2017).** *Irresistible: The Rise of Addictive Technology and the Business of Keeping Us Hooked.* Penguin Press.

   o Investigates the psychological mechanisms that make technology addictive.

10. **King, Daniel L., Delfabbro, Paul H., & Griffiths, Mark D. (2011).** *The Role of Structural Characteristics in Problematic Video Game Play: An Empirical Study. Cyberpsychology, Behavior, and Social Networking, 14*(3), 193-196.

- Examines features of technology and games that promote addictive behaviors.

Reports and Industry Studies

11. **Common Sense Media. (2022).** *The Common Sense Census: Media Use by Tweens and Teens.*

- Provides data on media consumption habits of younger demographics.

12. **Statista Research Department. (2023).** *Global Smartphone Penetration and Usage Statistics.*

- Insights into smartphone adoption rates and usage patterns across demographics.

13. **Deloitte Insights. (2022).** *2022 Global Mobile Consumer Survey: Trends in Mobile Usage.*

- Discusses the impact of mobile technology on consumer behavior.

14. **Pew Research Center. (2021).** *Social Media Use in 2021.*

- A comprehensive study on social media usage trends and their societal implications.

Technology and Mindfulness Resources

15. **Headspace. (2023).** *Mindfulness and Digital Well-being.* Retrieved from www.headspace.com.

- Offers resources on mindfulness practices to manage digital distractions.

16. **Freedom App. (2023).** *Blocking Distractions for Focus and Productivity.* Retrieved from www.freedom.to.

- A tool designed to limit screen time and digital interruptions.

17. **Calm App. (2023).** *Guided Meditations for Better Focus.* Retrieved from www.calm.com.

- Digital tools for fostering mindfulness and relaxation.

Web Resources and Articles

18. **TED Talks:**

- Adam Alter: *Why Our Screens Make Us Less Happy.*

- Cal Newport: *Quit Social Media.*

19. **Harvard Business Review. (2020).** *How to Manage Your Attention in the Digital Age.*

- Practical advice on regaining focus and productivity.

20. **The New York Times. (2022).** *The Case for a Digital Detox: Why We All Need to Unplug.*

- Explores the benefits of reducing screen time and embracing offline experiences.

Inspiration from Detox Practitioners

21. Personal accounts from interviews, testimonials, or surveys conducted with individuals who successfully undertook digital detoxes.

22. Quotes and anecdotes from mindfulness leaders like Thich Nhat Hanh and Eckhart Tolle on the importance of presence and intentional living.

About the Author

Elena Harper

Elena Harper is a mindfulness advocate, digital well-being coach, and the author of *Digital Detoxification: Embrace Balance, Presence, and Purpose in a Tech-Driven World.* With over a decade of experience in digital behavior analysis and a passion for helping others find harmony in the digital age, Elena has become a trusted voice in the fields of mindfulness and intentional living.

Born and raised in Portland, Oregon, Elena grew up surrounded by the beauty of nature, which later inspired her to seek balance between the natural and digital worlds. After completing her Master's in Behavioral Psychology from the University of Washington, she worked as a corporate consultant, studying the effects of screen time on productivity and mental health. Her findings led her to pursue a career dedicated to helping individuals reclaim their time and energy from the grips of technology.

Elena's workshops, blogs, and talks have empowered thousands to rethink their relationship with devices and social media. As a mother of two, she understands the challenges of navigating technology in both personal and professional spheres. Her insights stem not only from academic research but also from her own journey toward achieving balance in a tech-saturated environment.

When she's not writing or leading workshops, Elena enjoys hiking with her family, practicing yoga, and spending tech-free weekends exploring local art and culture. She is committed to helping others unlock their true potential by embracing mindful, purposeful living in the digital age.

Notable Achievements

- Founder of the "Mindful Tech Balance" initiative, which offers resources and courses on digital well-being.

- Speaker at international conferences on digital mindfulness and productivity, including TEDx events.

- Contributor to leading wellness platforms such as *Calm* and *Headspace.*

Disclaimer

The information presented in this book is for educational and informational purposes only and is not intended as professional advice. The author and publisher have made every effort to ensure the accuracy of the information; however, they assume no responsibility for errors, omissions, or any outcomes resulting from the application of the contents. Readers are encouraged to consult with a qualified professional for specific advice tailored to their situation.

Copyright

Legal Notice

This book is for informational and educational purposes only. While the author and publisher have made every effort to provide accurate and up-to-date information, they assume no responsibility for any errors, inaccuracies, or omissions. Any reliance placed on the information in this book is strictly at the reader's discretion and risk.

The content is not intended to replace professional advice, including but not limited to medical, legal, financial, or other professional services. Readers should consult with an appropriate professional for specific guidance related to their unique circumstances.

All trademarks, product names, and company names mentioned herein are the property of their respective owners. Their inclusion does not imply endorsement, affiliation, or sponsorship.

Unauthorized reproduction, distribution, or transmission of this publication in any form is prohibited without prior written consent from the author or publisher.

By reading this book, you agree to indemnify and hold harmless the author, publisher, and any affiliated parties from and against all claims, liabilities, losses, or damages resulting from your use of the information provided.